The Keys to Guinea's Development

Mamadi CAMARA

The Keys to Guinea's Development

Preface by Seydi Ababacar Dieng

L'Harmattan

Titre original :
Les clés pour le développement de la Guinée,
Éditions L'Harmattan, 2015

Translation from French to English
Done by Hélène du Preez

5-7, rue de l'Ecole-Polytechnique, 75005 Paris

http://www.harmattan.fr
diffusion.harmattan@wanadoo.fr

ISBN : 978-2-343-08236-3
EAN : 9782343082363

To my former students from the courses:

(i) Banking Techniques at the Institut Polytechnique Gamal Abdel Nasser in Conakry and

(ii) Macro-economics at the Cellule d'Etude de Politique économique (CEPEC) of the Centre national de Perfectionnement à la Gestion (CNPG) in Donka, Conakry.

ACKNOWLEDGEMENTS

This book was submitted to several people for observations, suggestions and advice. They all gracefully accepted to read it. I would like to express my deepest gratitude for their encouraging advice on all or part of the manuscript.

Ibrahima Soumah and Mamadou Doumbouya, former Minister of Mines and Geology and former Secretary General of the same Ministry, and El Hadj Mamadi Touré from the Head Office of the Compagnie des Bauxites de Guinée (CBG) rank amongst the greatest experts of the Guinean mining sector. They read the chapter on mining with great care, and this reassured me enormously.

I am grateful to Ousmane Tanou Diallo, Energy Consultant at the African Development Bank, who put at my disposal a wealth of information on energy in Guinea which was largely authored by him.

I also wish to thank Ousmane Conté, from the Research and Statistics Office of the Institut Monétaire de l'Afrique de l'Ouest (IMAO), in Accra, who edited the chapter on the Ghana Example.

I appreciate the availability of Mody Oury Barry, an electrical Engineer, who took the time to contribute to the chapter on hydroelectricity. I also thank Saloun Cissé, an acknowledged expert on the Guinean natural environment who edited the chapter on agriculture, as well as Sékouna Diakité, former official of the African Development Bank, who made meaningful general comments.

I wish to express my gratitude to Moussa Sidibé, a talented demographer of Guinea, who made relevant comments on the last chapter of the manuscript. I also thank Abdoulaye Touré, former national Director of the Plan. This expert in economical modelling and macroeconomic framing willingly edited the manuscript.

This book owes much to the quality of the editing, suggestions and comments by Mourad Labidi, former UN expert and Economy Consultant at the African Development Bank.

Finally, I wish to thank Seydi Ababacar Dieng, University Professor in Economics, Director of the economic and monetary research laboratory (Larem) of the Cheick-Anta-Diop University of Dakar (UCAD) and visiting professor at various universities, such as Sofonia University in Conakry. This author of several tribunes in the weekly Jeune Afrique, graciously accepted to write the Preface of this book.

TABLE OF CONTENTS

"Poverty is not an accident. Like slavery and apartheid, it is man-made and can be removed by the actions of human beings."

Nelson Mandela

PREFACE

This work by Mamadi Camara comprising of 14 well-organised chapters, is written in a pleasing reader-friendly style, due to the simple and intelligible approach adopted. It is based on a very rich and relevant documentation. The author's main concern is to find adequate and operational proposals to enable Guinea to irreversibly take the road to economic and social development in a context of social peace and political stability.

A staunch Pan-Africanist, he does not separate the future of Guinea from that of Africa. Therefore, he makes an objective assessment of the situation of the continent before focusing more specifically on Guinea. With the reflexes of the university lecturer – that he was – he strives firstly to explain very concisely the concept of development. Secondly, he outlines the reasons explaining the unequal development of countries, putting more emphasis on the specific case of African countries.

Focusing on Guinea since its independence, the author analyses it's economic, political and social situation in depth. This concise assessment is based on national and international statistics and on very precise examples. After presenting the strengths and weaknesses of Guinea and drawing inspiration, in particular, from the successful experiences of the countries of Southeast

Asia, he puts his concrete proposals on the table to initiate the development process of the country.

Starting with the five major natural assets of Guinea – "its mining, energetic, hydrological and agricultural potential and its access to the sea" – the author proposes a strategy which he calls "Transformation Strategy of Guinea (TSG)". This TSG is built on four pillars: agriculture, hydroelectric power, mining and good governance. It will promote human resources and subsequently the economic and social development of Guinea.

The author welcomes the current reforms since the advent of the 3rd Republic, in particular in budgetary and monetary management, and in the field of justice, and strongly urges the authorities to persevere in this way, and to implement the TSG.

In the last four chapters, the author recounts the experiences of Cape Verde, Ghana and Malaysia, and describes what Guinea will resemble in 30 years' time. The forward-looking dimension of the book reveals the author's strong optimism with regards to the future of his country.

Prof. Seydi Ababacar DIENG
Senior lecturer
Director of LAREM
Université Cheick Anta Diop

INTRODUCTION

As far back as 1962, René Dumont, a French agronomist, raised alarm bells when he published a book with a provocative, yet very prophetic title: "L'Afrique noire est mal partie"[1], (Black Africa has gotten off to a bad start) to draw the attention of African leaders to the bad start he noticed in the economic and social development processes of their newly independent countries. In this book he portrays the handicaps of the African continent, the problems linked to bad governance (corruption) and the difficult management of the cumbersome influence inherited from the colonial period. The diagnosis given then was very accurate. Indeed, the journey of most African countries shows these dysfunctions.

Developing countries (DC) are characterised, among others, by (i) low domestic savings, and (ii) dependence on one or two export products which are subject to fluctuations depending on the needs of industrialised countries. These characteristics have often placed the DCs in the position of applicants for capital to finance their economic development. These characteristics combined with misguided economic policies cause or increase the balance of payments imbalances.

---

[1] René Dumont, *l'Afrique noire est mal partie*, Editions du Seuil, Paris, 1962

Since the independence of African countries in the 60s to the present days, there have been many debates on their development that highlighted the existing divergences and convergences. However, the initiative of models for growth and economic development that were effectively implemented, in most cases, was notably left to Bretton-Woods Institutions.
From 1970 to this day, several formulas were proposed to African countries:

(i) to solve the temporary deficit of the balance of payments, the financial support provided by the IMF to the economic programmes of African countries operates within the context of a stand-by agreement (possibility of paying commitments in instalments) or a broad-based agreement to assist the Member State in overcoming its temporary balance of payments difficulties, or if need be, to support its economic reforms.

(ii) it has become increasingly apparent that the economic problems of African countries can only be solved in the medium and long term. The economic managers realised that the imbalances were not temporary, but structural in nature.

Therefore, it is imperative for these countries to set up substantial economic recovery programmes affecting both the supply and the demand; these programmes would be financially supported by Bretton-Woods institutions. Thus, faced with stand-by credit limits, a new paradigm came into being at the beginning of the 80s under the name Structural Adjustment Programme (SAP) which aimed at acting both on supply and demand, by stimulating structural transformations and rationalising public expenditure. These SAPs often encourage beneficiary countries to conduct austerity policies.

(iii) with SAPs results being largely unsatisfactory in most African countries, Bretton-Woods institutions proposed a new battle horse to combat underdevelopment and the fight against poverty which was introduced since the end of the 90s in strategic Poverty Reduction Strategy Papers (PRSP) and periodically updated. Reaching the completion point in the implementation process of the PRSP will allow great debt reliefs under the Heavily Indebted Poor Countries Initiative (HIPCI) and the Multilateral Debt Relief Initiative (MDRI)[2]. These reliefs provide sufficient budget room to allow the use of bold strategies to reduce poverty. At the same time, on the initiative of the countries and the United Nations' Development Programme (UNDP), the social aspects of development concerning health, education and ability to access natural resources have been upgraded to redefine the development concept.

In the mid-90s the UNDP introduced the notion of Human Development Index (HDI) taking into account certain parameters that had so far insufficiently been taken into account in the constituent parts of the social and economic development. Thus, the UNDP asked that the notion of development should not be limited to the creation of wealth represented by the Gross Domestic Product (GDP).

In addition, it may be recalled that in July 1990, during the high level Conference on Africa in Maastricht,

---

[2] The vast global movement in favour of indebted countries, called the Jubilee 2000 of the Church and started in 1996, has played a decisive part in the cancellation of the debt of poor countries by the intensification of its criticism of neo-liberal ideology and the programmes of the International Monetary Fund. The idea was that the year 2000 should be the year of the cancellation of debt. The movement forced the G7 to include poverty alleviation into the FMI economic programmes.

the limitations of the adjustment policies already became evident. Thus, it became apparent to all that the revival of the economies could not be generated by simply re-establishing the macroeconomic and financial balances, although these are essential.

As a result, it was considered at that time that the countries, without forgoing to manage the crisis, should at least adopt policies with long-term prospects, taking into account the demands of a future characterised by rapid change and growing uncertainty. The World Bank itself, in its report published in 2000[3], had admitted the inadequacy of adjustment policies and agreed that long-term prospects become the framework of sustainable development in Africa. The same idea was upheld, in the same year, by the UN Economic Commission for Africa (ECA).

It is within this context that a long-term prospective national education initiative and the creation of Future Africans in Abidjan were set up to help African countries to develop their Vision. At the Maastricht Conference, it was admitted once and for all that development is not possible if the transformations of behaviour, social and demographic, cultural and political structures, are not linked to purely economic measures, structured according to a specific vision and in a sustainable manner.

In 2000, another avatar emerged from the Millennium Summit that brought together 193 UN member states in New York, as well as 23 international organisations, namely the Millennium Development Goals (MDGs). The MDGs have set 8 targets for 2015, includ-

---

[3] Cf. 2000-2001 World Bank Report on development entitled "*Combattre la pauvreté*", World Bank, September 2000.

ing the reduction of extreme poverty and child mortality, as well as access to education. The latest assessment indicates that few African countries will reach these objectives, for lack of financial means, but also because of bad governance.

Within these initiatives taken by international organisations designed to promote the development of Africa, two originated in Africa itself:

(i) The Lagos Plan of Action (LPA) for the economic development of Africa in 1980-2000. The LPA that called for an endogenous development was aimed at an economic development based on self-sufficiency, cooperation and economic integration. However, the project was dead before it started due to lack of financing;

(ii) The New Partnership for African Development (NEPAD), which is an economic recovery plan for the African continent, adopted by Heads of States in 2001 during the OAU Summit in Abuja. NEPAD became the socio-economic development programme of the African Union in 2002 at the end of the Durban Summit in South Africa. It includes major infrastructure projects aimed at eradicating poverty and reaching the Millennium goals. Its objectives are very ambitious, namely an average of 7% growth rate per year in African countries.

However, as for the LPA, the implementation of this great continental project suffers from a lack of financial resources. In fact, domestic savings and the strengthening of revenue collection that are considered as essential resources for the implementation of the project are insufficient. And the rich countries' commitment, taken in Monterrey in March 2002 by G8 member countries, to increase public development aid (PDA) with US$12 billion[4], per year from 2006, has not been sufficiently honoured, nor has the commitment of the European union to double the PDA between 2004 and 2010, from 34.5 billion Euros to 67 billion (i.e. the equivalent of US$85 billion during 2005) of which at least 50% of the increase intended for sub-Saharan Africa[5]. However, in defence of donor countries, it must be noted that the international financial crisis that started in 2008 and shook the foundations of the economies of the developed countries, and to some extent, the subsequent control of their citizens, have certainly had an impact on the increase in the volume of public debt. Furthermore, the private capital flows, in terms of foreign direct investments (IDE) in Africa that were also relied upon, were insufficient for Sub-Saharan Africa.

The implementation of these various development schemes in the last 50 years did not produce much of the expected results, such as the establishment of basic sustainable infrastructures and a meaningful reduction of poverty. Although Africa seems to have progressed in the last ten years with an average growth rate of 5% per year (between 2000 and 2007, it has grown by an average of 5.5% per year)[6], Henri de Raincourt and Donald Kaberuka give the following reasons to this failure to produce expected results:

(i) these patterns were designed exogenously; (ii) their implementation is often biased and incomplete;

---

[4] From the Lagos Plan of Action (LPA) to NEPAD: two conceptions of development, two ideologies… by Célestine ZANOU, in La Presse du Jour of 12 December 2008.

[5] See: Area of interest 1: Funding for Africa's development.

[6] See: New tools to finance the challenges of a new Africa, by Henri de Raincourt, Minister of Cooperation, and Donald Kaberuka, president of the African Development Bank, in Le Monde of 25/04/2011.

(iii) the various developing stages in African countries pose adjustment problems that are not always adequately understood by experts from international financial institutions; (iv) their adoption by African government was insufficient.

What should be done to develop Sub-Saharan African countries effectively? This is a complex issue, though not insurmountable. With political will, an internally designed clear vision and a coherent programme of structural projects could open the way to a real economic and social development of African countries. In terms of development, everything that is done should be designed first, then rigorously implemented, and finally assessed to appreciate the results. However, good governance is undoubtedly the essential ingredient of the above-mentioned elements, even though other factors must be taken into account such as the impact of the international context and external partners.

We are more and more convinced that expenditures in (i) health (constructions, hospital equipment, health centres, clinics, family planning, training of medical personnel), (ii) education (building and equipping of schools, training of teachers), (iii) infrastructures (building of roads and communication routes that promote the development of trade and the expansion of markets and stimulates economic growth, and also building of electricity, water and sanitary networks), all contribute to economic and social development.

International financial organisations and African Governments have learnt much from negative experiences accumulated on the path of growth and development, as well as from cases of good practice. These experiences should inspire more policies of socioeconomic development designed internally and implemented with the aid of bilateral and multilateral donors, and with the help of direct foreign investors.

In this respect, the aim of this book is to propose points of reflection on the strategic actions to consider for Guinea specifically, and on the economic policies to be implemented to help the country overcome its lethargy and offer future generations the living conditions to which the country's economic assets entitle them.

CHAPTER ONE

THE CONCEPT OF DEVELOPMENT

Definitions are generally simplistic and do not fully cover all the aspects of the defined word. We substitute various explanations to encompass all aspects of the concept.

"Development is at first a somewhat ambiguous, hardly operational concept, in any case as long as it is not qualified"[7].

The notion of development has developed over time from a more pronounced quantitative content to a higher qualitative content. Nowadays, economists make a distinction between growth and development.

Growth is usually considered as the percentage increase of the Gross Domestic product (GDP, i.e. all the goods and services produced in a country in one year). François Perroux[8] defines economic growth as "*the sustained increase of GDP for one or more long periods*".

Development is the transformation of economic structures, as well as social, cultural, political and insti-

---

[7] *Guinea's population: current situation and future challenges*, Ministry of Planning and UNFPA, Editions Ganndal.

[8] François Perroux (1903-1987) PhD in Economics was a professor at the Law faculty of Lyon, then at Science-PO and at the Collège de France.

tutional structures that accompany and explain this growth. François Perroux defines development as "*the set of mental and social changes of a population that enables it to increase, cumulatively and sustainably, its real global product.*"

Development is also "the transformation of demographic and social structures that generally accompany growth. We insist here on the structural aspect (industrialisation, urbanisation, salarisation, institutionalisation, etc.) and on the qualitative aspect (changing mentalities, behaviour patterns, etc.) of long term evolution."[9]

For his part, Paul VI considers that "*Development cannot be limited to mere economic growth. To be authentic, it must be integral, that is, it has to promote the good of every man and of the whole man.*"[10]

The GDP is the most commonly used indicator to evaluate development. However, considering the inadequacy of this aggregate for measuring the quality of development, the UN programme for Development (UNDP) introduced in 1990 a new indicator called the human Development Index (HDI) based on three elements: health, education and access to natural resources. However, HDI having limitations, UNDP experts created a new indicator in 1997, namely the human poverty index (HPI) based on three elements: life expectancy, education level (measured by the literacy rate) and life conditions, i.e. access to health services, drinking water, and child malnutrition.

---

[9] See: *Dictionnaire d'économie et de sciences sociales*, 7th revised and expanded Edition, by C.D. Echaudemaison, Editions Nathan, Paris, 2007.

[10] See: Paul VI, Populorum, 1957.

According to Amartya Sen[11], "Human development, as an approach, is concerned with what I take to be the basic development idea: namely, advancing the richness of human life, rather than the richness of the economy in which human beings live, which is only a part of it".

All these definitions include the idea of "progress", a progress measured by the improvement of life conditions that is not merely a higher standard of living, but also: "a reduction of drudgery and working time, improvement of housing, better access to culture and information, a higher education level, changes in the role and status of women, improvement of qualification and health, etc."

Are the variables taken into account in the development themselves insufficient? This has led to the notion of sustainable development which "*combines economic, social and environmental needs*"[12]. Sustainable development is a type of development that best addresses the needs of the present without compromising the capacity of future generations. Sustainable development wants to preserve natural balances and ensure to future generations a quality of life equivalent at least to that of previous generations.

If we take all these elements into consideration, we notice that since the industrial revolution of the 19th century, the gap between the per capita income of the richest countries and that of the poorest countries has increased constantly. In 1870, the richest nations were

---

[11] Amartya Sen is professor in Economics at the University of Harvard. He was a Nobel Prize winner in economy in 1998 for his contribution to the establishment of human development indicators.

[12] See: Madagascar: For a dialogue on development challenges, World Bank, June 2013.

11 times richer than the poorest. In 1995, they were 50 times richer. In 1998, the UNDP notes in its annual report that the assets of the richest men is larger than the total GDP of sub-Saharan Africa. In spite of the dynamism displayed by some emerging countries, such as China, India, the tigers of Asia and Brazil, the gap between developed and undeveloped countries is still increasing, leaving the poor countries behind.

Generally speaking, a country is considered to be developed when its per capita income is higher or equal to US$ 20 000. However, this definition must be relativized, since other considerations arise to distinguish between industrialised and developing countries (for instance, Libya has a per capita income of US$ 21 397, but is not considered developed). With the majority of Sub-Saharan African countries having a GDP inferior to US$ 1 000, the idea of getting the seconds to catch up with the firsts is a gigantic task. However, African countries show great disparities in their development, some of them registering double-digit growth rates, thanks to their oil riches or good governance.

Since the second half of the 20th century, several successive development strategies were followed, set up by Governments and international institutions. For comprehension purposes, we can distinguish two main periods: from 1950 to 1980; and from 1980 to the present.

The national development strategies: failures and successes

During the first period, there were three main strategies: First, the industrialisation strategy chosen by newly independent countries after decolonisation, with the State having a central role in a context marked by the opposition between the capitalist western bloc and the socialist eastern bloc. The idea at the heart of this strategy is that the growth of the industrial sector will help other sectors of the economy expand because of the weight or technological progress of the sector that is the driving force. Thinkers like Ragnar and Paul Rosenstein-Rodan or François Perroux and Albert Hirschman advised the firsts to invest in all industrial sectors, or the seconds to invest mainly in the drivers of the economy ("François Perroux's growth poles").

Industrialisation through import substitution was born in that period. This strategy called "desarrollism" from the Spanish *desarrollo* which means development, spread throughout Latin America and was theorised by Raul Prebisch. It was used in the 1950s by most developing countries, in particular in Latin America, Asia (Korea, Philippines, etc.) and in Africa (Senegal, Kenya, etc.). The desired effect in this type of industrialisation is to lead to an industrial production in partnership with the internal market. In other countries, like India in the 1950s and Algeria since 1967, the State plays a major part in directing investments (five-year plans in India since 1948), substituting itself for the market. This option is Soviet-inspired. However, at the end of the 1970s, the result of these strategies was that "they did not lead to a sustainable growth and development process; poverty and inequalities are still a reality."[13]. This failure is due to the small domestic market and the necessity to import technologies and capital goods to ensure industrialisation, yet it led to an important deficit in the balance of payments. Furthermore, since 1982, sev-

---

[13] See: *Analyse économique et historique des sociétés contemporaines*, Philippe Deubel, Pearson Education, France, 2008.

eral Latin American countries have experienced what was then called the "debt crisis".

However, we must point out that a large group of DCs is following another industrialisation strategy by promoting an outward-orientated development based on the export of their natural resources, such as petroleum and agricultural or mining products. The rationale behind this type of industrialisation is that the financial resources obtained from these exports make it possible to import capital goods to promote the industrialisation of the country. However, this strategy has proved counterproductive due to the deterioration of the terms of trade. Yet, the countries that promoted exports by substituting primary products with increasingly sophisticated products have been successful. This was the case with (i) Hong Kong and Singapore in the 1950s, and South Korea and Taiwan in the 1950-1970s, these four countries having become the "Asian Dragons"; and (ii) countries like Brazil, Chili or Mexico in Latin America.

In general, there are more failures than successes. This is the reason why, since 1989, Samir Amin speaks of the failure of Africa's development efforts[14].

The interventionism of the Bretton-Woods Institutions

Given the failure of the development strategies of the DC highlighted by the debt crisis of the 80s, international institutions, in particular the IMF and the World Bank, joined the debate by proposing structural adjustment programmes (SAP) with conditionalities. These liberal-minded policies had an effect both on domestic

[14] Samir Amin, *La faillite du développement en Afrique et dans le tiers-monde. Une analyse politique, Editions l'Harmattan, Paris 1989.*

demand (consumption, investment, variation of stocks) and supply (production system), through stabilisation policies and the implementation of structural measures that can modify substantially the DC's economic organisation. The American economist, James Williamson has qualified these structural measures of "Washington consensus" based on three principles of conditionalities: liberalisation, privatisation and deregulation.

But, ..." *the enforced dismantling of the public service, the reduction of public health or education expenditure imposed by budget balance criteria cause major set-backs in terms of literacy or child mortality in African countries. The burden of debt increases and reduces correspondingly the resources intended for the human development of the population. In general, the SAPs have been beneficial in countries already advanced in their development which had stable political and social institutions*"[15].

During the financial crises at the end of the 1990s and at the beginning of the third Millennium, countries, even those looked upon as development models by the BWI experienced set-backs: Mexico in 1995, Russia in 1998, Brazil in 1999, Argentina in 2002 and especially Thailand, Indonesia, Malaysia and South Korea in 1997 following the collapse of the Thai currency (the bath) due to a "too rapid and unbridled financial deregulation". Joseph Stiglitz, an American economist and recipient of the Nobel Prize in economics in 2001 and former Senior Official of the World Bank, considers that the BWIs have a solely liberal conception of development through what he calls "market fanaticism", a model they

[15] See: Philippe Deubel, booklet already quoted.

believe can be applied to all countries, whatever their development level and their economic and social structures.

New Paradigms

In view of the limits of the liberal system, it would be helpful to think further to put development in a context taking into account parameters that were kept in the background up to now. Thus, we reshape the "Washington consensus" in order to add additional elements: establishing good corporate governance, fighting against corruption and creating "a safety net" through social security, and also fighting against poverty (defined as the common objective by the IMF and the World Bank in 1999). Thus, "*in September 1999, the IMF put the fight against poverty at the heart of its activities in low-income countries, by replacing the enhanced structural adjustment facility (ESAF) with the poverty-reduction and growth facility (PRGF)... The participatory process applied in order to draw up the poverty reduction strategy paper (PRSP) is the most important innovation of the new facility. All the low-income countries wishing to obtain a loan from the IMF or World Bank or secure debt relief under the heavily indebted poor countries initiative (HIPC) are preparing this document. For this purpose, the national authorities rely on broad consultations with the stakeholders, including civil society and donors, rather than negotiating directly with IMF or World Bank services. The aim is to integrate poverty assessment and ways to combat it in official macroeconomic policies" (IMF 1999). However, these adjustments do not challenge the ultra-liberal foundation of the "Washington consensus".*

Joseph Stiglitz proposes to extend the concept of development by including non-economic dimensions such as access to culture, democracy, education, health and the reduction of inequalities. He emphasises particularly *" the crucial role the State must play in the development: need for more representative and participating institutions (including reconsidering the political independence of central banks), complementarity with the market in the production of public goods (reconsidering privatisations)...*"[16].

Amartya Sen, the Indian economist, adds a philosophical dimension to the concept of development. To him, "development strategies should not only focus on the production of revenues and resources to ensure development, but also of capabilities, i.e. each person must have the capacity to lead a decent and meaningful life. This fulfilling life requires the guarantee of certain functional "capabilities" such as being able to avoid dying prematurely, having access to secondary education, but also having access to all human emotions (laughing, crying), enjoying oneself, etc.". Sen's works would form the basis for the establishment of the human development indicator to which he greatly contributed. He even considers that democracy is one of the prerequisites for development. However, this is debatable considering that some countries managed to develop themselves under enlightened dictatorships (South Korea in the 60s under the leadership of President Park).

Finally, development strategies would form part of what we call sustainable development. This concept emanating from the Stockholm conference in 1972 was

---

[16] See: Philippe Deubel, booklet already quoted.

updated in 1983 when a world commission on environment and development, created by the UN, published a report entitled "Our common future" in which it considers that the exploitation of natural resources and environmental degradation are a danger for future growth and development. However, closer scrutiny shows that industrialised countries are more responsible for environmental degradation and climatic change than developing countries. Why then should developing countries be submitted to very restrictive policies to repair the damage caused by rich countries?

The international Community went even further by adopting in September 2000, in New York, the "Millennium Declaration", designed to achieve a set of 8 objectives by 2015, which few African countries will be able to achieve within the deadline.

A study by Simon Johnson, Jonathan Ostry and Arvind Subramanian ("JOS") published in 2010 in IMF Staff papers, entitled "Prospects for Sustained Growth in Africa: Benchmarking the Constraints", which although it had other objectives, offers an insight on past development strategies. "In the last four decades, a dozen countries in the world that are called the SG group (Sustained growth) in JOS's study, have registered periods of rapid and sustained growth, – these are Chili, the People's Republic of China, the Dominican Republic, Egypt, Indonesia, Korea, Malaysia, Singapore, Taiwan, Thailand, Tunisia and Vietnam."

In their analysis, the authors have also divided African countries into two groups: 19 countries are registered in the first group (GSSA for Growing SSA), which is a heterogeneous group (large and small countries; costal, insular or landlocked countries; oil and non-oil producing countries; with various languages; in the north, south, east and west of the continent) comprising Angola, Botswana, Burkina Faso, Cameroon, Cape Verde, Chad, Equatorial Guinea, Ethiopia, Ghana, Guinea, Lesotho, Liberia, Mali, Mauritius, Mozambique, Rwanda, Sudan, Tanzania and Uganda. They have enjoyed an average growth of GDP per capita higher than 2% during the decade preceding the survey (1996-2005). The other group comprises sub-Saharan countries that do not meet these requirements, including Madagascar"[17]. As for sub-Saharan countries, they have not had sufficient growth to significantly reduce poverty.

[17] See: Madagascar: Economic Update, October 2012, the World Bank Group – Antananarivo Country Office.

CHAPTER TWO

WHY ARE SOME COUNTRIES RICH AND OTHERS POOR ?

Professor Mancur Olson, of Maryland University, USA, tried to answer this question during an international workshop on rural infrastructures, organised by the World Bank on 19-23 May 1997, in Washington DC.

Olson's thesis challenges certain ideas circulated in economic theory based on the abundance of natural resources. We will try to reproduce here his thought process.

It is generally agreed that under-development is due to three types of shortages or deficiencies, which are bottlenecks in the implementation of development policies of poor countries.

Firstly, there is a lack of natural resources. This can be assessed by the very high ratio of population compared to the scarce amount of natural resources. This view is based on the example of Asian countries that are highly populated.

The second constraint lies in the fact that domestic saving is very low in developing countries (5% of the GDP); therefore, capital may be scarce.

Finally, the last handicap is the lack of human resources and know-how, without taking into account certain cultural and religious attitudes that could hinder economic development. At a certain time it was considered that religions like Hinduism or Buddhism are detrimental to development.

Therefore, the key to development is to put sufficient input in developing countries to bring about almost mechanically economic growth.

However, according to Olson, the above-mentioned factors do not stand up to a closer analysis of the true reasons for some third world countries' inability to create enough wealth to meet the needs of the people.

Overpopulation is a valid reason in Asian countries, but not for some African and Latin American countries where depopulation is obvious in certain regions.

Then, it must be noted that the number of inhabitants per square km is higher in Germany than in India, the second most populated country in the world.

As for the natural economic potential, we cannot explain the economic development of Japan, Taiwan or Germany by an abundance of natural resources.

There remains, however, the lack of capital and of domestic savings that hinder economic development. Yet, these two factors are not given naturally; and we cannot oblige third-world countries to save beyond their capacity to finance the economic and social development.

If we refine the analysis, we can say that given the inadequacy of their own financial resources we may ask why capital is not directed where it is needed the most.

Indeed, capital looks for places with the highest possible profitability. Yet, capital owners are always investing on the New York, Tokyo or London financial markets, i.e. places that already have abundant financial resources, even a certain saturation.

Why don't they turn towards markets where there is a lack of capital, i.e. underdeveloped countries instead of looking for investment opportunities in saturated financial markets?
These are huge capitals running into US$ 10 000 billion that are badly needed by developing countries (DC) to finance their economic and social development.

The third set of factors to examine critically is human resources and the competence of human capital that is lacking in DCs.

In order to do this, we will consider the borders between countries as a criterion. We take note that a less developed country can have common borders with a more developed country. This is the case with Mexico and the United States of America, the two Koreas or the two Germanies before reunification.

Why do adjoining countries have such diverging standards of living and different human capacities and technologies?

When looking at national borders, we realise that Germans earns ten times more than Haitians. The former live in a prosperous and successful country, while the latter in a very poor country.

Yet, when they leave their respective countries to go to the Unites States of America, the difference between their incomes diminishes as if by magic. The Haitian earns in the United States more than half of the German's income.

Thus, when going over the border, the German's productivity becomes very high. The difference in income between the two persons when they are in their country of origin can not only be explained by the difference in competence, know-how and level of training.

After examination, Olson believes that the three above-mentioned factors do not withstand a critical examination.

We must therefore acknowledge that the key determining factor of the wealth or poverty of nations depends on the way they are governed and the coherence of their institutions with the defined policies and those in force.

Therefore, the lack of competent human resources is not the sole Gordian knot, since the Haitian example demonstrates that institutions and the clarity of the rules of the game that bring about a tenfold increase in workforce performance.

It is even less the lack of natural resources, since the examples of the spectacular development of Japan, Taiwan and Korea debunk this thesis. We can also mention Guinea that has a wealth of natural resources but in the 50 years of independence has been incapable of launching itself economically. Indeed, Guinea is a country generously endowed by nature due to its hydrologic, agricultural and mining potential (bauxite, iron, gold, diamonds, titanium, limestone, uranium, manganese, graphite, etc.). The country has the world's largest reserves of bauxite estimated at 50 billion tons, which will ensure a production for 25 centuries at a rate of 20 million tons per year. The country also contains oil deposits.

In addition, the lack of capital in the DCs can be compensated by the attraction of good governance on the enormous capitals looking for profitable investments. If the developing countries managed to mobilise only a small part of the capital, they would not need financial resources from the World Bank.

The task of intellectual elites and international institutions such as the International Monetary Fund, the World Bank and the African Development Bank, is to ensure that bad governance in terms of discipline, transparency and equity improve in developing countries.

Once this prerequisite has been met, foreign capital will flow in naturally, human and intellectual capacities will flourish freely and the possible lack of natural resources could be turned into an advantage.

Therefore, the political and institutional environment is very important in the performance of an economy. Government must create and manage such an environment of commitment to development, which is lacking in most developing countries.

The creation of an institutional environment enables each economic agent to develop their full capacity and guarantee greater opportunities for all.

Indeed, the State must create a competitive environment for economic, private and public economic operators. And to win the battle of development in record time, the leadership must commit itself firmly and resolutely to achieve the objectives. He must be the catalyst and the facilitator of development and be very ambitious.

This is the great issue that the participants, meeting in Kampala on 15-18 August 1997 to discuss the question, "States and Markets: What can we learn from Asia?" learned from the experience of Korea and Malaysia. The direct involvement of the leadership in the industrialisation process of these countries was the factor that guaranteed success.

Of course, no experience, however successful it may be in a certain country, can be transposed to another country. Therefore, the main rapid growth factors of

South-East Asian countries can only be an interesting source of inspiration for the African countries facing the difficult problem of development in an international economic environment affected by the crisis. They must make the best of it through developing strong institutions and consolidating the parameters of the rule of law, to create a favourable environment conducive to the development of the private sector that will one day be the driving force of economic and social development.

This tendency can already be noticed in some sub-Saharan African countries which benefit from a "good governance premium". This is the case for Ghana and Cape Verde which as a result of the stability of their institutions and the foundation of democratic change of government, have benefitted in the past few years from a substantial flow of financial resources enabling them to acquire strong socio-economic infrastructures.

CHAPTER THREE

WHY DOES GUINEA REMAIN A POOR COUNTRY?

Guinea has advantages that other countries could be envious of, and great potential in terms of natural resources.

It has enormous natural resources which are important assets for the socio-economic development of the country. Indeed, the country has five major natural assets that, if they had been exploited sooner, would have enabled it to become a middle-income country. They are its mining, energetic, hydrologic and agricultural potential as well as its access to the ocean.

The mining potential[18] is enormous. The main mineral resources are bauxite (2/3 of the world's bauxite deposits), iron ore, gold and diamonds. This list is far from exhaustive since all the mineral wealth has not been registered yet.

The energetic potential is huge. According to estimates made between 1978 and 1989, there are 129 potential sites for hydroelectric dams on the following rivers: Konkouré, Cogon, Bantal, Kakrima, Fétoré, Ka-

[18] See: Revue de la Chambre des Mines de Guinée, Register 2006, year 2007, Republic of Guinea. See : Journal de l'Economie guinéenne, No 18/19, January 2005.

ba, Soukoudoukoura, Bafing, Dundouko, Kokoulou, Komba, Mamou, Sankarani, Niger, Niandan, Lolo and Diani.

The rainfall is one of the major assets of the country. Guinea has an abundant rainfall estimated at some 400 billion m3 per year, with 350 billion m3 divided between runoff, evaporation and infiltration.

The land potential is estimated at 364 000 ha of land that can be developed for a great variety of crops. It has many rivers and a rich variety of vegetation.

Finally, Guinea is a coastal country with a 300km coastline with 3 ore ports in Kamsar, Conakry and Benty, as well as a freight port and a fishing port in Conakry.

In spite of this strong natural potential, the country has not managed to launch itself successfully to reach a significant level of development. This would have enabled the people of Guinea to enjoy a much better quality of life than they do now.

"*Thus, mining activity has not resulted in substantial economic and social progress; the availability of arable land and water has not achieved food self-sufficiency; the energetic potential has not generated enough electricity to serve homes and promote the industrialisation of the country; the autonomous harbour of Conakry has not developed sufficiently to become a remedy in the sub-region for imports and exports of land-locked countries such as Mali and Burkina Faso*" [19].

"The transformation of its natural potential in material wealth faces several constraints, mainly the insufficiency of energy production and low agricultural

---

[19] See: Mamadi Camara, *Où va la Guinée?*, Editions l'Harmattan, Paris June 2010.

productivity, the low level of human resources and most of all, bad governance" [20].

The financial bad governance reached very high levels during the transition period, from 2008 to 2010. In this period of time, the contracts conducted by direct agreement represented 91% of the total procurement contracts, and the proportion of extra-budgetary expenditure came to 80% of the budget in 2010[21]. The sum total of the over-the-counter agreements concluded in the last two years represent about 13 000 billion Guinean francs (US$ 2.2 billion), i.e. 44% of the GDP[22]. The government did not respect any normal procedural rule in public expenditure. The isolation of the country during this exceptional period due to sanctions combined with the suspension of external aid, led to a rise in the cost of living.

In general, the economic evolution of Guinea in the last decade has been characterised by fluctuating economic performances, with periods of "*economic growth which could potentially reduce poverty and on the other hand, periods of economic crisis that would increase it*" [23].

[20] See: Mamadi Camara, booklet already quoted, page 19.

[21] See: Guinea, Assessment report of the Economic and Financial Reform Support programme (PAREF), African Development Bank, March 2011.

[22] See: Guinea, Country Strategic Document 2012-2016, African Development Bank, prepared by ORWB.

[23] See: Poverty and inequalities in Guinea from 1994 to 2012, Analysis from surveys among households, Ministry of Planning, national Planning Directorate, July 2012.

The landmark study of the African Development Bank:" Infrastructures and Growth in Guinea" [24] (validation in November 2011) had identified six weaknesses, some of which are still valid today. They are: (i) the escalation of conflicts in the sub-region (Ivory Coast, Guinea Bissau, Liberia and Sierra Leone); (ii) the high level of corruption; (iii) the employment situation; (iv) the problems linked to drug trafficking in the sub-region; (v) income inequalities; and (vi) food insecurity. To these elements of instability we must add others that are not less important, namely: (i) the conflict marking relations between the Government and opposition parties, especially when fixing election dates and modalities. These tensions often turn into street protests leading to violence and instability; (ii) the poor diversification of the economy; and (iii) the outbreak of the Ebola epidemic in 2014, a disease with a very high fatality rate.

The regained stability in the sub-region, especially in Ivory Coast and Liberia, together with the restoration of technical and financial partners has created a favourable environment for economic recovery. At the domestic level, the current reforms taking place since the coming of the 3rd Republic are moving in the right direction. For instance, there is a more rigorous fiscal and monetary management. As far as justice is concerned, some very encouraging steps have been taken, in particular: (i) the establishment of the High Judicial Council; (ii) the special status of magistrates (that should protect them from corruption); (iii) the establishment of criteria for the appointment, deployment and promotion of Magistrates;

---

[24] See: Guinea: Country strategic Document 2012-2016, prepared by ORWB, African Development Bank, 26 January 2012.

(iv) the strengthening of the penal system; and (v) the creation of the national Directorate for access to law and justice.

Furthermore, the cleaning up of public service records that brought to light some 5000 shadow officials[25], and the improvement of the monitoring of recruitment have enabled the State to make significant savings.

However, the challenges remain the same:

- How can we boost the economy to create enough employment and wealth to bring the country to the level of prosperity it should have with its natural resources?
- How can we turn the huge potential of the country into material wealth that would benefit the whole population?
- How can we turn the four assets identified above that are real gifts of nature and unparalleled economic advantages for the prosperity of the country?

[25] See: Guinea, DSP 2012-2016, booklet already quoted.

CHAPTER FOUR

THE SYNDROME OF POVERTY IN GUINEA

In the last decade Africa has made huge progress. Overall, according to available sources, the continent has had a GDP growth rate of about 5% per annum between 2003 and 2013. However, this performance, mainly based on mining activities and service development, did not benefit the majority of the people, considering that oil and mining revenues benefit primarily political leaders and foreign companies. Thus, the result of the growth acceleration has been very low on the most disadvantaged sectors of the population. Poverty has not declined significantly.

Indeed, in Africa, the percentage of people living on less than US$1.25 per day has only decreased from 56.5% in 1990 to 48.5% in 2010. At the same time, South Asia has seen its poverty prevalence rate decrease to 31% in the same period, while South Asia and the Pacific reached 12.5, Latin America and the Caribbean 5.5%; and North Africa and the Middle-east 2.4%[26].

With a demographic growth of 3.1% per annum, the Guinean population is estimated to be at around 11.3 million inhabitants in 2012, with 52% women and 48%

[26] See: Growth for all is possible, *in* Jeune Afrique No 2765 of 5-11 January 2014.

men. Out of this population, 55.2% live below the poverty line against 43% in 1996. With the poverty line fixed at 8.815 GNF (New Guinean Franc)[27] per person per day at 2012 rates, the number of poor people in this period has gone from 4 million to 6.2 million[28]`. Thus, poverty seems to have increased during the last 15 years.

The poverty phenomenon is mainly concentrated in rural areas due to the fact that the population living under the poverty line amounts to 63% against 31% in urban areas. However, these figures do not reflect the tragedies occurring in people's daily lives, especially in the countryside. Behind these figures lies the tragedy of poverty.

You just have to examine a certain number of indications in the lives of urban and rural inhabitants to realise the seriousness of their situation.

Makeshift housing, promiscuity, health and poor income

<u>*In towns*</u>

Hygiene in some houses is very precarious due to a lack of sufficient toilets for all the people in towns. Promiscuity puts a strain on the respect of modesty between father and children and brothers and sisters. However, when you are poor, you have to tolerate all these situations without complaining, since you have to

---

27 There are about 7 000 Guinean new Francs in US$1.

28 See: Poverty and inequality in Guinea 1994-2012, Analysis from surveys among households (Preliminary version), Ministry of Planning, National Statistics Institute, June 2012.

live with the means at your disposal, no matter how scant they are.

In the suburbs of Conakry, on a visit to the Bonfi district, I noticed that a 60 year old man lived with his wife and his 11 children (three boys and eight girls) in two rooms. His furniture consisted of two old armchairs that were turned into beds for some of the children in the evening. A torn and bleached curtain hung at the front door. At night fall when everyone slept, they would wake up to certain scenes that they could easily have done without in normal circumstances. But what can you do when you are poor?

The low household income does not allow them certain basic amenities such as a comfortable bed and mattress, a house with separate rooms for the sexes. Besides, poor households have difficulty obtaining and paying for the services they receive. The supply of electricity does not meet the demand of the people of the capital; therefore there are long periods of load shedding. However, this family does not have access to electricity during the rare periods when it is available. In addition, water is stored in cans or pails.

Poverty has a negative impact on people's health, making it unable to cope with health expenditure.

Thus, to illustrate such a situation, I witnessed at the UTM of Donka a scene demonstrating the difficulty some families had to pay hospital fees. A man and his wife brought their infant to the children hospital to be treated. Since they were not able to pay the doctor's fees and the prescribed medicines after the consultation, the medical practitioner not only did not ask consultation fees, but gave the parents some money to pay for the prescription he had written out, thus showing charity that is unfortunately not often recognised.

In villages

In Upper Guinea, in a village situated 85 km from Kankan, I saw some things that speak volumes on the state of poverty of rural populations.

In this village, the home is a thatched hut of banco. The furniture inside is very basic. It is usually a bed with a straw mattress, and a few stools or, on the rare occasion, chairs. The poorest (they are the more numerous) have a banco bed (bili in Malinké) with a straw mattress. The back door of the hut opens generally on the "bathroom", a space in the open surrounded by a straw fence where one washes with a pail of water. In cold or hot weather this open space serves as bathroom. And in some areas of Upper Guinea winter can be cold in December and January.

Although, in the last few years some houses with tin roofs have appeared in the villages, huts are still prevalent.

To light up the huts at night, the peasants use hurricane lamps or medieval lamps (Fitinan in Malinké). Torches from China have a rosy future, since they are still currently used in the 21st century in the towns and villages of Guinea,

In this general picture, children live under very precarious conditions. Suffering undoubtedly from malnutrition, they are skinny with protruding bellies, and red hair the colour of dust. Most of them do not wear shoes, and wear threadbare and dirty partly torn clothes. Some children have a cold and cough, but are not treated. What do the people do when someone is seriously ill in the village? The patient is taken by bicycle or motorbike to the prefecture, 10 km away, where there is a health facility. Since there is practically no other means of transport in the village, there is much risk in transporting a very sick patient on such a long distance with these two means of transport.

This absence of medical facilities is not only in villages. It is found all over Guinea. In general the hospital equipment is so ancient that patients who can afford to pay for services go the clinics and hospitals of Conakry that are mostly places of death; and the wealthier go to Senegal or the Maghreb countries to be cared for.

EBOLA: FROM SANITARY CRISIS TO ECONOMIC AND SOCIAL CRISIS

The first person contaminated by the virus, "patient zero", was a 2 year old child who died on 6 December 2013, a few days after he became ill, in a village of Gueckedou, in the Guinean forest region. And one week later the virus had killed all those who had been in contact with him: his mother, his 3 year old sister and his grandmother. Since the beginning of the Ebola virus epidemic in Guinea in December 2013, the sickness has taken a heavy toll in the country, with a thousand dead people by the end of October 2014.

The outbreak of the disease has exposed the weakness of the health infrastructures to cope with such a disease that took everyone by surprise, and showed the lack of decent hospitals, well-equipped research laboratories, sufficient logistic means and equipment in health facilities. It also revealed the scarcity of qualified medical personnel. In addition, illiteracy and traditions, relating in particular to burial rites, have contributed to spread-

ing the disease.
Yet, besides the health crisis, the Ebola virus epidemic has become an economic and social crisis with unpredictable effects on the economic evolution of Guinea. According to World Bank estimates, a loss of one or two percentage points of the estimated GDP growth of 4.5% in 2014 is expected. Similarly, the progress realised in the fight against inflation that was at the single-digit level, may be reversed, with an increase in the cost of some food stuffs such as rice. The disruption of agricultural activities in the areas affected by the epidemic and the closing of the borders with some countries will contribute to the scarcity of some products in the markets and a loss of revenue for traders. In addition, the interruption of air services to Guinea by most airline companies, the departure of investors, especially in the mining and industrial sectors, will have disastrous consequences on employment, the mobilisation of financial resources, tourism (the hotel occupancy rate has dropped to 10-15%), and actual investments (potential investors prefer waiting for a time after the Ebola epidemic). Finally, it should be noted that the epidemic has led to an exodus, forcing the government to rethink its anti-poverty strategy by viewing the eradication of the epidemic as the highest priority.
The international community has taken action to assist Guinea, to enable the country to control the disease and reduce its adverse impacts on its socio-economic evolution. Thus, it is of the utmost importance to seize this opportunity to use all the donations in a rational way to not only control the epidemic, but also to improve existing health facilities and build those needed. This is a good time to equip the health sector in a sustainable way to enable it to cope with any other contingency in the

future.

Sources: Magazine Espoir 13 World Bank and author's personal research.

In villages, the limited diet has a negative effect on people's health, in particular on children. The food consists usually of rice with a sauce that is so clear that you can see yourself in it, and consequently it cannot contain the necessary nutritive elements needed for the healthy growth of children; vegetables and animal protein are often lacking. Sometimes, the meal consists only of "to", a dish of fonio and cassava usually eaten with a gombo sauce. Owing to the lack of a diversified diet, mothers continue breast-feeding their babies until they are 2 or 3 years old. This results in very slow growth, and most of the children look younger than their age.

For decades, official statistics have said that women in Guinea have 5.6 children. This average is misleading. In fact, birth-rates remain uncontrolled in villages, and women can have 7-8 children. These frequent pregnancies have a negative effect on mother and child. In general, the mothers live in the same hut as their children, boys and girls, some of them lying on mats on the floor, because of a lack of funds to be able to build another hut.

The low income brings about solidarity among peasants. In fact, in a village, it is customary for those who have lost a relative to receive the condolences of the inhabitants of the neighbouring village. On the day of the funeral, delegations arrive. After the usual blessings for the soul of the departed, the head of each delegation announces its village contribution. In 2005, some villages gave 2000FG (1US$ = 7000 GNF on the parallel market, exchange rate November 2012), as a contribution from the heads of the families of a village. These contributions were not even worth a dollar. Yet, in these conditions of extreme deprivation, what the bereaved family appreciated most was the fact that these delegates often walked several kilometres to grieve with the deceased's family. Poverty is also the severe lack of money among rural populations.

Low income obliges peasants to walk to the fields, even if in the mining regions of Upper Guinea, there are more and more motorcycles with sometimes too many mortal accidents.

To go to the fields, most peasants walk for kilometres. Women generally go on foot. In addition, they also have to do hard domestic work, especially pounding rice, dry manioc, mil, maize, etc. by hand. In some villages small crushing mills are appearing. However, hand piling has not disappeared everywhere yet, due to a lack of financial means and organisation.

Schooling at risk in Upper Guinea.

Another key development is the low enrolment in schools among the children of the villages of Upper Guinea, owing to the fact that the majority of them are working in the fields to help feed the family. Schools are empty most of the time.

For instance, I heard in this village situated in the Sabadou-Baranama sub prefecture, the story of a ten year old little girl, called Sogbé. This friendly, polite girl was required by her mother to look after her one year old baby sister while her father and mother went to work in the fields. As an impromptu baby-sitter, she was condemned to not attending school because she had to look after the youngest daughter.

There is only one teacher in the school and he is taking great licence in performing his teaching functions as he is frequently absent from school. In fact, the teacher goes to Kankan to stay with his family two weeks out of four. The lack of authority in the system enables the teacher to give his classes when he feels like it. Teachers' absenteeism is very common even in urban areas, including the capital city, Conakry.

Moreover, with the uncontrolled artisanal mining of gold mines in some regions of Upper Guinea, especially in Siguiri, parents simply remove their children from school to go and look for gold. This growing phenomenon has serious consequences, especially on the health of the gold-diggers, the environment, natural resources and socially. In fact, artisanal exploitation " contributes to deforestation, soil-degradation, air-pollution by dust and carbon monoxide, soil and water pollution by used motor oil and chemicals (used batteries containing manganese and lead, abandoned in the pits), the loss of biodiversity, the deterioration of the landscape, etc.". It can also cause respiratory problems and often fatal accidents in the pits. One of the consequences is the lack of schooling of the children who will not get an education. Fields are also abandoned for the gold mines, which delays the food self-sufficiency the country has been aspiring to since independence. Finally, it must be noted that there is moral depravity on the mining sites contributing to the propagation of sexually transmitted diseases.

These practices will have disastrous consequences on Guinea's future if appropriate policies and strategies are not implemented. In fact, human capital is the first and foremost resource for a nation wanting to meet development challenges. If Guinea is overtaken by the progress of other countries on the continent, it will find it difficult to bounce back. Because it will be too difficult to make up for lost time and get to the level other countries have reached by investing greater technical, financial and material means in education. All the emerging countries have used quality human resources to reach a higher level of development. Natural resources, no matter how plentiful, mean nothing if there is no qualified workforce to process them.

Poverty is a human tragedy, a handicap that slows down or impedes the growth of the affected people. In order to lift half the population of Guinea out of poverty, government must improve the education system, strengthen the infrastructures needed in a modern country: drinking water and sanitation, electricity, make farming more attractive, provide a better organisation of artisanal mining (gold), better equipped health facilities, modern housing, all-season roads, telecommunications, etc.

The various poverty symptoms in Guinea and the main weaknesses of the country give an indication of the strategy that should be implemented to accelerate the economic and social development of the country, by focusing on several pillars to support it.

CHAPTER FIVE

THE TRANSFORMATION STRATEGY OF GUINEA

For over 50 years Guinea's development depended essentially on extractive economy. However, mining exploitation has not enabled Guinea to reach the development level that corresponds to its huge natural resources. For 56 years (1858-2014), the growth rate peak never reached the 6% set during the formulation of "Guinea, Vision 2012" in 1996. Even worse, poverty increased with a prevalence rate from 43% in 1996 to 55% in 2012[29].

Therefore, it is imperative to diversify the economy by relying of course on the mining industry, but also and especially on agriculture, the hydro-electric potential and governance.

The transformation strategy of Guinea (STG) should aim at the effective diversification of the economy and a better management of public resources. It has a very strong foundation with a good enabling environment for agriculture, a powerful hydro-electric potential and huge mining resources. Agriculture, hydroelectricity and mines can pull the economy and drag with them other

---

[29] See: Poverty and inequality in Guinea 1994-2012, Analysis from surveys among households (Preliminary version), Ministry of Planning, National Statistics Institute, June 2012.

sectors of economic growth, provided that a certain code of ethic governs the resources generated.

Yet, before any development process, the safety of people and property should be guaranteed; otherwise any qualitative change in the people's lives will be in vain. When the safety of the citizens is secure, people can enjoy their assets. Because, sleeping peacefully and going about their occupations the next day without fearing being shot down at home or in the street are the most precious advantages in a person's life.

Besides safety, any development must rely on growth accelerators such as education, health and road infrastructures. Without quality education, peasants cannot take complete ownership of the development process.

Certain countries with poor natural resources have managed to reach a high level of development through training. This is the case for Japan and Asia. And this is specially the case of Switzerland which, with no natural resources, is today the 8th economic power in the world in terms of revenue per capita, and the biggest exporter of chocolate in the world although it does not cultivate any cocoa beans on its territory[30]. A small land-locked country (about 41 000km2 with 8 million inhabitants) Switzerland has developed a work ethic behind its large exports, including clocks, luxury watches and of course chocolates. Switzerland's economic performance is due to its capacity to create a diversified economy based on human capital that has reached a very high level of expertise in watch-making, the chocolate industry, banking, etc.

[30] See: BMF warns SA economy far from transformation goal, by Zandile Luphahla, in The New Age, Thursday, 19 June 2014.

A country can develop without abundant natural resources, but without quality human resources its potential for economic development remains poor.

Over the period 2007-2012, Guinea has spent an average of 12% of the national budget on education. This is insufficient for the training needs at all levels of the education cycles[31].

Without a high quality of public health, it is a utopia to believe in fast sustainable development in African countries. Ensuring people's health, makes it possible to have a workforce that keeps factories running and increase agricultural production. The high level of HIV/AIDS causes some African countries to lose a percentage of their GDP. For the period 2007-2008, Guinea allocated an average of 2% on health, while the Abuja Commitment to Action[32] asked that 15% of the State Budget be allotted to health care[33].

The third growth accelerator includes transport infrastructures that are essential to ensure the disposal of production and the flow of goods to the sales facilities and harbours for coastal countries. They are also essential for the easy movement of people.

While taking into account all these important factors, any development strategy of Guinea must rest on the

---

[31] See: Strategy Document for the Reduction of Poverty DSRP III (2013-20150, Department of Economy and Finance, Permanent Secretariat for the Poverty reduction Strategy (SP-SRP), May 2013.

[32] See: During the Special Head of State Summit held in Abuja on 26-27 April 2001 to meet the challenges of infectious diseases such as HIV/AIDS, tuberculosis and other related infectious diseases, the Governments committed themselves to allocate at least 15% of their annual National budgets to the health sector.

[33] See: DSRP III 2013-2015.

four above-mentioned main pillars that are the economic and social development levers.

The idea is to continue exploiting mining resources, while at the same time develop the agricultural and hydro electrical sectors and improve governance. The strategy is not to stop at the mining sector, but to have a vision that encompasses the main growth engines.

The four pillars of the development strategy of Guinea are: improvement of agricultural production, upgrading of the hydro-electric potential, a more effective exploitation and transformation of mining resources, and improvement of governance and capacity building.

First pillar: improving agricultural production

Interest in this sector is due to the fact that it harbours the majority of the people, as well as the poorest people of Guinea (about 63%)[34]. The second reason is that studies have shown that the growth of GDP based on agriculture is both efficient in reducing poverty and developing activities other than agriculture. "*In China's case, it has been noted that growth based on Agriculture was 3.5 times more efficient in reducing poverty than growth outside agriculture, while in Latin America it was 2.7*"[35]. All the countries that managed to put an end to hunger had first improved their agricultural production, as exemplified by the green revolution of the 60s implemented in India.

[34] See: Guinea's population: current situation and future challenges, Ministry of Planning and UN Funds for the population, Editions Ganndal, May 2013.

[35] See: Agricultural sector strategy of the African Development Bank Group 2010-2014, 7 December 2009.

The target set in the Agricultural Development national Policy Letter, phase 2 (LPDA-2) assumed reaching rice self-sufficiency by 2005. This target has obviously not been reached; on the contrary, imports have increased with 54% from 2000 to 2007.

More recently, Government adopted the National Agricultural Investment and Food Security Programme (PNIASA) for the period 2012-2016. This programme aims at improving agricultural productivity and food security, so that Guinea becomes a food-exporting country. It provides for public resources limited to research and outreach, and looks for investment from the private sector. Government has prepared an ambitious action plan to tackle agriculture and make it play a bigger role in social and economic development. It also provides for the development of agricultural commodities.

In the agricultural sector, the livestock sub-sector, source of animal protein, has not been developed sufficiently. Yet, it has a strong potential.

Second pillar: upgrading of the hydro-electric potential

For various reasons, Guinea's hydro-electrical potential has so far not been sufficiently exploited, in spite of all the favourable conditions enjoyed by the country: abundant rainfall, presence of many rivers and catchment areas. There is such a huge potential that achieving it would boost not only growth, but Guinea would be able to export electricity to the neighbouring countries of West Africa.

Therefore, it is imperative to invest in this sector because, without electric power, any economic and social development effort is threatened by the risk of failure. As a matter of fact, the development of the other sectors depends on the availability of sufficient electric power. This is the reason why the current energy deficit undermines the country's economic, social and cultural progress.

Third pillar: exploiting and using mining resources more efficiently

Since Guinea's independence, the mining sector has generated growth and being the sole source of export revenue, has contributed to budgetary resources more than any other sector. Yet, has the mining sector produced all the expected results? Wouldn't it be necessary to use export revenue more efficiently if we want the mining sector to contribute more meaningfully to reducing poverty?

Fourth pillar: improving governance and building capacities

Without good governance, the efforts made in the other three pillars will be doomed to failure because factors like the lack of coordination, the demobilisation of energies and corruption destroy the gains.

The four pillars are analysed in the following five chapters; the first pillar (improving agricultural production) includes a subchapter (developing stock farming) to which a whole chapter has been dedicated.

CHAPTER SIX

FIRST PILLAR: IMPROVEMENT OF AGRICULTURAL PRODUCTION

Guinea is capable of feeding its population

In general, in Africa, most of the people live from agriculture or related activities. According to the World Development Report, 2008, 70% of the people living in Africa work full time in agriculture. In spite of that, the African performance in agriculture remains poor compared to Asia. As a matter of fact, while the per capita growth of the people living from agriculture in Africa is less than 1%, it is 3.1% for Asia and the Pacific region. In Africa, this growth results more from the increase of cultivated areas than from an increase in productivity. Out of 54 African countries, only 9 invested 10% of their budget in agriculture[36]. Yet, in 2003, the Maputo Commitment required African governments to allocate 10% of their national budget to agriculture.

---

[36] See: "Scaling up agribusiness should be Africa's next growth frontier", in Business Report International, Johannesburg, South Africa's Financial Daily, page 18, Thursday, April 17, 2014. Carlos Lopes is the Executive Secretary of the UN Economic Commission for Africa in Addis Ababa.

The most well-known *success story* is the green revolution in India in the 60s. The tragedy of the great famine in 1943-1944 which, according to some sources, killed 3 to 4 million people was still a vivid memory when India got its independence in 1947. The great famine in colonial India was due to the combination of two factors: the grain deficit and the context of the Second World War that caused the British colonial power to give little attention to food-related issues.

The green revolution is a technological package which includes: (i) varieties of selected high yielding rice and maize seeds; (ii) irrigation or management of the water supply; (iii) the use of fertilisers and pesticides; and (iv) adequate management capacities.

In addition to this package, independent India implemented a strategy based on research and the commitment of the political leadership, scientists who worked on selected rice and maize seeds, bureaucrats and farmers themselves. They all participated with an open mind and were men of action who applied a strategy that was clearly outlined in advance. The result was that India never suffered starvation again. Cultivated land was increased from 1.9 million ha in 1960 to 15.5 million ha in 1970, 43 million ha in 1980 and 64 million ha in 1990. And in 1975, India produced 10 million tons of cereals[37].

The challenge to improve African agriculture is twofold: water must be managed and there must be a regular supply of agricultural inputs. African soil is in some places old, impoverished and washed away. Human ac-

---

[37] See: Good news India. From famine to plenty, from humiliation to dignity. November 2002. The statistics used come from documents of the Indian Institute of Science.

tivity is the cause of these scourges (shifting cultivation, soil acidity, and rapid decomposition of organic matter due to too much sunshine). According to the *World Development Report*, 2008, 16% of the soil has a low nutrient content, while this percentage is only 4% in Asia. Yet, the use of fertilisers is only 8kg/ha, and even less compared to the projected goal of 50kg/ha in terms of the African Summit on fertilisers held in 2006. In addition, the GDP of several African countries is heavily dependent on the rainfall. The frequent alternation of floods and droughts is very detrimental to the quality and quantity of the agricultural production.

Moreover, African agriculture is affected by the poor road infrastructure and the bad management of soil conditions. Thus, 50% of the farming population in Asia live within one hour's walk from the local market, while about 50% of African farmers live 5 hours or more away from a market.

Guinean agriculture

Guinea has all the conditions necessary for a flourishing agriculture. As a matter of fact, according to estimates, 6.2 million hectares are cultivable, i.e. 25% of the national territory. Yet, only 1.6 million hectares are exploited, which leaves a high extension capacity of cultivated areas. In addition, the hydro-agricultural potential is estimated at 180 000 hectares with 157 000 ha of plains and 23 000 ha of lowlands. In the countryside, each inhabitant has an average of 3.8 ha of farmland[38].

---

[38] See: Guinea's population: current situation and future challenges, Ministry of Planning and UNFPA.

Famers grow several varieties of food crops. Rice is in the first position as it occupies 41.7% of cultivated areas and 80% of the farmers cultivate it. In 2008-2009, the rice production was estimated at 1 400 000 tons of paddy. However, the country imports 300 000 tons per year which, according to the FAO, leaves a deficit of 436 000 tons in 2008. Overall, 23% of the rural population lives at the margin of food insecurity. However, in Guinea nobody is starving. Apart from rice which is the staple food, the farmers cultivate maize, millet, cassava, peanuts, potatoes, fonio, yams, sweet potatoes, taro and citrus fruit.

On average, the annual growth of the agricultural sector is estimated at 4%, and even 5% in 2011. Yet, this rate is low considering that with the annual demographic growth being estimated at 3.1%, the agricultural production will not be able to cover the population's needs in the long run. Thus, the performance of the agricultural sector is poor. The contribution of agriculture to the GDP has been decreasing constantly from 90% before independence to 62% in 1971, 46% in 1988 and less than 20% in 2012. The share of agriculture in exports has decreased from 90% in 1958 to 7% currently[39]. Agricultural products represent 11% of exports. Guinea exports mainly coffee, cotton, rubber (after Liberia, Nigeria and Côte d'Ivoire), bananas (5000 tons in 2010, far behind Côte d'Ivoire which produced 250 000 tons)[40], fruits and vegetables.

---

[39] See: Africa: history, economy, politics 1998-2001, Agriculture in Guinea at the beginning of 2000, by Olivier Bain, article put on line again by Jean-Marc Liotier.

[40] See: The state of trade in West Africa, annual Report, 2012.

Under the combined impact of the excessive attention to the mining sector at the expense of others, of bad governance and outmoded cultivation techniques, the agricultural sector, in spite of fertile soil, did not develop sufficiently to prevent the country from importing huge quantities of rice after 56 years of independence.

"*A National Census of Agriculture was conducted in the campaign of 2000-2001, within the context of the World programme for the Census of Agriculture 2000 advocated by the FAO, for the national censuses of the decade 1996-2005 in order to develop a fairly complete appropriate data base on the main agricultural issues at national and regional level. This census produced several lessons, especially the fact that the peasants farm on small parcels of land and are still using rudimentary implements. Out of the total number of cultivated land in 2000, 18.4% of the plots have an area of 1 to 1.5ha. The areas larger than 5ha represent 4.2% of the total cultivated areas*"[41]. Therefore, agriculture has basically not changed, it remains essentially subsistence agriculture.

Agricultural work is done manually on traditional farms. The clearing of land, upkeep and harvest are done 99% by hand, ploughing 82% and sowing manually on 96% of cultivated fields. In 2000, out of 2 272 638 cultivated plots representing 1 370 145 ha, only 20% received organic and/or mineral fertilisers. The majority (94%) of cultivated areas in traditional farms used unselected local seeds, and practically no plot of land used crop protection products. The proliferation of nema-

[41] See: National Agriculture census (NAC: 2000/2001). National Agricultural Statistics Service (SASS), Republic of Guinea.

todes and other parasites significantly reduced the output per unit area.

A rudimentary agriculture has rather low yields: for rice, an average of 1.7 tons per hectare for 2000-2008 against 1.95 tons per hectare in Africa in 1989, while the high yield rice tried in China yields 7.3 tons per hectare (i.e. 948 kg more than ordinary rice) in the Shanggao district, in the Province of Jiangxi[42]. For maize, the average is 1.50 tons per ha; for fonio paddy, 1.10 t/ha; for peanuts, 0.7 t/ha and for cassava 7 t/ha. These averages are based on estimates by SASS on outputs[43].

The productions from 2002 to 2008 are based on estimates. According to SASS estimates, "the rice production amounted to 865 242 tons in 2006, 911 413 tons in 2007 and 953 083 tons in 2008. These tonnages are highly inferior to the population's food requirements".

Thus rice is Guinea's main agricultural industry; it covers 80% of farms, meets 65% of cereal requirements and employs 37% of the labour force. According to projections based on the simulation model of Guinean economy (MSEGUI), the rice production will manage to meet the food requirements of the country, between 2017 and 2018.

The agricultural sector has large areas of hitherto unexploited arable land. The soil is so fertile that each natural region can by itself feed the whole of Guinea. The variety of climates and soils enables the country to develop several sectors and to promote the diversification of the economy. All that is needed is to take two major

---

42 See: Le Quotidien du Peuple *online*, Edition of 16-10-2007.

43 See: Table entitled Dynamics of Production of major Food Crops from 2000 to 2015, SASS, Ministry of Agriculture and Cattle-breeding.

pro-active measures: train a sufficient number of agricultural officers, ensure water control and assess fertility of the soil to make specific corrections possible.

As a matter of fact, "*the way to go for agricultural policy, is to develop food crops by taking into account at least three parameters: (i) providing aid to peasants by supplying them with quality seeds and fertilisers and crop protection products; (ii) securing water control because too much or too little water often ruins farmers' efforts; and (iii) improving the business climate to create the necessary conditions for the emergence of a class of great farmers who will be able to produce cereals and speculation products for export*".

Trained agricultural agents will constitute a body of agricultural technicians capable of assisting peasants in the different regions. This assistance will focus essentially on (i) disseminating innovative farming techniques that will increase productivity; (ii) disseminating high-yield shorter season seed varieties, fertilisers and crop protection products; (iii) grouping peasants in co-operatives so that they will be able to rent tractors in turn to plough their fields and decrease the drudgery of work in the fields.

Water control is essential to develop agriculture. Very often, too often in fact, farmers' efforts are ruined by the excess or lack of water. With Government's aid, water storage projects will have to be created in order to irrigate cultivated areas according to cereal requirements. The farmers, who have an empirical knowledge of the natural environment, will be able to use these water facilities effectively.

When both these conditions are met, agricultural statistics services will have to be used to assess from a base year and over a certain number of years, the results obtained, season after season, by farmers exploiting the land.

In this way, the best practice cases in terms of yield will be duplicated in the other farming areas where the output was poorer.

The farmers should be able to make a contribution towards buying a small machine to pound rice or cassava, maize, even Shea nuts. This system will considerably reduce the harsh work of women after the harvest. The time gained by women will enable them to plant vegetable gardens and sell their produce (tomatoes, onions, cucumbers, etc.) on the markets.

The development strategy of the agricultural cluster will be implemented into three phases: (i) working upstream by helping farmers better by supplying them with agricultural inputs; (ii) controlling water; (iii) reducing the drudgery of ploughing by using a tractor wherever the nature of the soil allows it; and (iv) using devices to pound the cereals; and (v) establishing an agricultural land policy[44]. If this strategy is properly implemented, Guinea will be able to feed itself and even export food.

The implementation of this strategy started in 2011, when Government distributed 20 000 tons of fertilisers, 1 500 tons of rice seeds, 500 000 litres of crop protec-

---

[44] It is very important to take into account the economic policy of the soil when developing land policies and reforms related to land ownership. As Dr. Joan C. Kagwanja notes in his presentation on the "improvement on a great scale of land investments governance in Africa: the role of parliamentarians", there are many elements including land security, the establishment of a land policy, land reform, women's land rights and ownership rights, forced expulsions, the management of natural resources, the informal settlements, land disputes and conflicts, etc.

tion products and 150 tractors to peasants to produce an extra 100 000 tons of rice.

This policy had immediate effects on the agricultural production and the price of rice fell sensibly on the markets of the capital, Conakry. As a matter of fact, the price of 1 kilo of rice went from 9 000 GNF in 2009 to 6 000GNF in 2012, i.e. a decrease of almost 33.33%.

If the control of water were guaranteed, the rice production would be much higher owing to the fact that floods and lack of water often ruin farmers' efforts.

Apart from the increase in output, water control, the use of fertilisers and the distribution of improved seeds, that which ensures proper development of the agricultural sector, is the improvement of rural infrastructures. By rural infrastructures we mean rural and community roads, the commercialisation, storage and processing of the agricultural production, the water used in agriculture and water storage, and the other infrastructures for cattle, fishing and rural energy. All these elements have been identified as being a priority in the Agricultural Sector Strategy of the African development Bank for 2010-2014.

Government must, together with organising economic actors in the industrial and commercial sector, encourage the organising of agricultural operators by facilitating their access to bank credits in order to promote a network of modern and efficient farmers.

Government must also ensure that agricultural products be processed locally, to create a strong agro-industrial embryo capable of processing agricultural products locally, in order to get considerable added value. As Carlos Lopes said, history teaches us that agriculture, in particular the developed sectors of agro-industries and agro-business, has been the engine of economic growth in countries all over the world, from Brazil to China. Agro-business was the key to meeting the demand of food products, especially processed products[45].

For the African Union, 2014 is the year of agriculture and food security. This is the opportunity for African countries and Guinea in particular to strengthen the political commitment of African leaders in favour of agriculture in order to give it new dynamics. Guinea is one of the "good students" in its commitment to the Maputo Agreement of 2003 to channel 10% of public expenditure to the agricultural sector (agriculture, cattle breeding and fishing), with the country having devoted 14.5% of the national budget to agricultural investments in 2008.

---

[45] See: Carlos Lopes, article already quoted.

CHAPTER SEVEN

SUB-PILLAR: DEVELOPMENT OF LIVESTOCK

Guinea is the bastion of a race of ruminants adapted to the ecological conditions of a sub-humid zone[46]. They are the *Ndama* cattle, *Djallonké* sheep and goats whose genes enable them to resist the diseases endemic to this area, such as trypanomososis, endoparasitosis and dermatophilosis. These unique genetic characteristics have developed exclusively in West African habitats such as Guinea. Moreover, these animals have other particularly interesting attributes which enable them to adapt to the prevailing ecological conditions of the sub-humid region, such as high levels of humidity and poor quality feeds[47].

From the Fouta Djallon Highlands which is the original home of the local indigenous livestock, they have spread gradually to other countries, in particular Senegal, Gambia and Mali which have large numbers of in-

[46] I recently provided a short outline of all the hidden potential of this branch, with the collaboration of a cattle-breeding expert who knows Guinea well, where he undertook several missions. He is Souleye Kitane, official at the African Development Bank, Regional Office of Dakar.

[47] See: Maurice Houis, *La Guinée française*, Editions Maritimes et Coloniales, 1953.

digenous ruminant livestock. In the areas surrounding Guinea, these races of cattle have sustained high genetic erosion due to cross-breeding. In Guinea, most of the livestock is made up of those hardy breeds which are a valuable genetic treasure, if we take into account the viability and diversity of genetic resources of global significance.

Breeding is practised in a variety of forms: (i) sedentary family livestock farming, combined with agriculture, is characterised by small herds with a total of less than 10; (ii) semi-pastoral activities with herds of 10-30 which are usually sedentary but become transhumant during the dry season; (iii) extensive pastoral stock-farming which is transhumant, with a number of cattle larger than 30 and combined most of the time with small ruminants. For small ruminants the most important system is basic extensive breeding with an average of 10 animals. There is also the semi-urban family livestock farming with an average of 5 animals which are fed on household waste [48].

In 2010[49], Guinean livestock was estimated at 4.9 million heads of cattle, 1.6 million goats and 1.9 million sheep. More than 90% of these consisted of endemic livestock with at least 50% being pedigree livestock. The livestock contribution to the GDP in Guinea has decreased from 4 to 2% between 1980 and 1990. This decline does not point to a regression in this sector but

---

[48] See: Abdoul Goudoussi Diallo, Geography of Guinea, L'Harmattan, Paris, 2011, page 72.

[49] See: Investor Forum paper in Abu-Dhabi FP Livestock, Agriculture GAD, December 2013, "Investment opportunities in livestock breeding (hatchery, livestock feed production, abattoirs, selection and cross-breeding).

rather to a lack of dynamism and a significant growth in other sectors (mining, fishing, services). In 2010, its contribution rose to 20.9% of the agricultural GDP and 4.6% of the national GDP, with an average annual growth rate of 3.8% in the period 2007-2010. According to estimates it should reach a 5.4% rate between 2011 and 2014.

However, the development of the breeding sector is crippled by the lack of pastoral space, the difficulties of supplying zoo-technical and veterinary inputs, the loss of workforce to the mining sector, in particular the gold rush in the region of Siguiri, the lack of a national policy for the genetic improvement of local breeds, etc.

In spite of this sector's potential, Guinea has to import meat to feed its population. This deficit is due to the lack of structure in the animal value chain. Estimates highlight an annual per capita availability of 12.6 litres of milk, 7.7 kg of meat and 0.56 kg of eggs, while the food security targets are 15 litres, 15 kg and 1.4 kg, respectively.

The initiative aimed at promoting the breeding of indigenous ruminant livestock coincides with favourable circumstances in West Africa and in the world. As a matter of fact, several countries in West Africa currently experience a high demand in pure breeds of indigenous cattle for cross-breeding in order to improve the resistance of their livestock to tropical diseases. Furthermore, the emergence of the mad cow disease caused by breeding focused on production of the North and its transgression of the animal food chain (livestock fed with animal bone-meal) has brought about new dietary habits based on the search for a more natural diet. These circumstances offer excellent opportunities for indigenous livestock breeding which can now favourably position itself in international markets. It should be remembered that indigenous livestock products (milk, meat, hides) are natural because they come from a natural production which uses essentially the fodder from the natural pasture of the livestock.

The institutional organisation of the breeding sector in Guinea is the responsibility of the Livestock Breeding Ministry. It promotes stock-farming activities, the development of animal production and the improvement of animal health. In each administrative region, there is a regional development and planning office including rural and environmental development cells. In the prefectures, there are prefectural directions for rural and environmental development. The sector has a network of private veterinarians and strong socio-professional organisations which play an important part in the development of livestock breeding.

Guinea also has an Agricultural Research Institute whose main mission is to promote agricultural research, including livestock breeding. In 1981, with the support of the FAO and the PNUD, the country established the Breeding Support Centre (CAE) of Boké which is the spearhead of research on endemic ruminant livestock. The centre harbours a basic herd which is the product of a selection process in a facility, but also uses a network of pilot breeders who have pure Ndama breeds from a selection process in a facility.

The low cost of production makes breeding indigenous livestock profitable. The animals graze in the natural pastures and only need a supplement at the end of the dry season. The production process may be longer but it follows the natural meat constitution principles without the inappropriate use of chemical or bacteriological products. The production cycle spreads over 3 to

5 years, but at 2 years already males can be processed as meat and yield an average of 90 to 100 kg per animal. The meat quality and organoleptic characteristics make it possible to sell meat cuts at very profitable prices. This is the reason why the breed and breeding methods must be preserved while at the same time modernised with a commercial touch to improve the marketing of the products. Efforts to structure the sectors, modernise the production chain to be able to trace products and focus on the commercial quality, will lead to the improvement of the Ndama cattle meat, Djallonké goat or sheep meat in the international market.

Structuring of the sector should result in the emergence of new segments in the supply chain (cutting plants, modern butcheries, refrigerating plants at the harbour and/or at the airport for exports).

The first step is to attract a specialised clientele through meetings at agricultural shows in other parts of the world, at forums on livestock products and through direct contact with livestock product distributors in the countries of the North.

In this sector, research plays an essential role in the identification of pure breeds, the preservation of information on the subject and the determination of optimal conditions of production, while maintaining a natural production system. Government must proceed with its efforts to increase animal production, with the introduction and dissemination of fodder in traditional stock-farming from the breeding support centres of Boké and Famoïla (Beyla). This programme was strengthened within the framework of the Programme of Sustainable Management of Endemic Livestock in West Africa (PROGEBE). Moreover, the programme "Vaccines for neglected diseases (VACNADA)" aimed at vaccinating over 60% of the small ruminants in 2011[50].

Development prospects for large ruminant breeding are promising. First of all, it is an activity performed on a large scale in at least three natural regions of the country (the Foutah, Upper-Guinea and the Guinea Forest Region). The authorities are determined to supervise stock breeders by vaccinating the animal population and saving the environment to maintain the quality and abundance of pastures.

A further advantage of stock-farming is that oxen are still used for ploughing, especially in Upper Guinea; cow dung is also used as fertiliser in vegetable gardens and is used to plaster the huts in several regions of Guinea owing to its thermal virtues.

---

[50] See: Annual macroeconomic framework 2011 (Implementation of the Poverty Reduction Strategy). Ministry of Planning, National Planning Directorate.

CHAPTER EIGHT

SECOND PILLAR: INCREASED VALORISATION OF HYDROELECTRIC POTENTIAL

Without energy, development is an illusion.

The use of electrical energy is still low in Africa, especially in Guinea. The per capita consumption of energy in Africa (including, hydroelectric power, fossil fuels and biomass) currently represents one quarter of the world average[51]. The percentage of the Guinean population having access to electricity amounts to 18%.

Yet, Guinea's hydroelectric potential is significant and is worth exploiting to obtain maximum economic profits.

The first aspect of this potential is the structure of the ground and the rainfall. "The volume of rainfall is estimated at 450 billion m³ per year, a third of which is usable, 25% goes to the sea and the rest will irrigate the large territories of the sub-region"[52]. Even if these figures have noticeably diminished, they are still meaning-

[51] See: Pedro Lopes: "Scaling up agribusiness should be Africa's next growth frontier", in Business Report International, Johannesburg, Thursday, April 17, 2014.
[52] See: Booklet quoted above

ful compared to other countries of the West African sub-region. As a matter of fact, "with an estimated water potential of 27 000m³ per capita per annum, Guinea is rated as one of the countries with the most water in the world."[53]

The second aspect of this potential is the abundant water supply, from 1165 permanent streams spread all over the national territory, which are between 6 and 660km in length with catchment areas from 6 to 71 000km² [54].These numerous rivers make of Guinea the "Water tower" of West Africa. Besides these surface waters there is a reserve of over 12 billion m³ of subterranean water in Guinea[55]. With a water potential estimated at 27 000m³ per capita per annum, Guinea is one of the countries with the most abundant reserves of water on the planet[56].

Guinea is a member of four (4) great waterway organisations in Africa: ABN (Niger Basin Authority), OMVS (Organisation for the Development of the Senegal River), OMVG (Organisation for the Development of the Gambia River) and Mano River Union. All these organisations are located around the great rivers which have their source in Guinea, namely the Niger, Senegal, Gambia and Mano Rivers.

---

[53] See: Guinea: DSP 2012-2016, African Development Bank.

[54] See: National workshop on medium-term public spending, Energy sector (Electricity, Renewable energy, Water, Fuels), Ministry of natural Resources and Energy, Republic of Guinea, 1997.

[55] Report on Guinea's economic and social situation (2009-2011), Ministry of Planning, National Planning Directorate, Conakry, November 2012.

[56] See: M3 Holdings, Most Economical Alternative Energy Solutions: Combination of "Green Energy" and "High Quality Water", 2 May 2014, Sandton, South Africa.

The third aspect of this potential is the large number of dams with more than one hundred listed, including micro-dams, medium-sized dams and large dams. Moreover, these dam sites are distributed in the four natural regions of the country. However, those exploited thus far are not full because the rainfall is not as abundant as in the past. Nevertheless, the hydroelectric potential is estimated at over 23 000 GWh (6 000 MW) [57]. This capacity surpasses Guinea's needs, and could therefore provide tremendous opportunities to export surpluses.

In the revised master plan for the means of production and transport of electrical energy of the Economic Community of West African States (CEDEAO), the characteristics of 19 dam projects have been determined on the basis of the latest studies on each project. They are the following dams: Amaria, Bonkon Diaria, Diaraguéla, Fetor, Fomi, Franknedou, Grand Kinkon, Gozoguézia, KassaB, Kaléta (currently being developed by the Guinean Government), Kokbédou, Kouravel, Kouya, Lafou, Morisakano, Nzébéla, Poudalbé, Souapiti and Tiopo[58].

Other dam projects, namely Digan, FelloSounga, Balassa, Boureya, Diaoya and Koukoutamba are part of the portfolio of the Organisation for the Development of the Senegal River which originates in Guinea.

Of all these dams, those of the Konkouré complex are the most powerful in terms of installed capacity:

---

[57] See: Booklet already quoted.

[58] See: Table 23 – Hydroelectric projects – Investments data (1/2) *in* A major asset for the valorisation of Guinea's hydroelectric potential. Le système d'échange d'énergie électrique ouest-africain (EEEOA)/ West African Power Pool(WAPP), 2012.

Souapiti (515 MW); Amaria (300 MW); Grand Kinkon (291 MW) and Kaleta (240 MW). The construction of these dams requires large financial resources which must be pooled as part of regional projects. Souapiti, for instance, needs an investment of US$ 1 344 per kW for a total investment cost of US$ 692 million, and will produce guaranteed energy of 2 403 GWh/year. In order to make these projects profitable, their exploitation must be linked to the needs of the mining industry which is a great consumer of energy. According to some estimates, an aluminium plant with a capacity of 200 000 tons per year would create an additional requirement of 3 000 GWh/year[59]. It is estimated that the demand for electricity by the mining industry will be 800 MW by 2025.

The establishment of the Souapiti, Amaria, Kaléta and Fomi complex on the one hand, and of the projects of interconnection of electricity networks on the other hand, will turn Guinea into a country with high capacities of energy production and exportation in the West African sub-region[60].

According to various sources[61], the average access to electricity, at national level, is around 18%, in spite of this energy potential. Thus, over 80% of the Guinean population do not have access to electricity and those in the cities experience long and frequent load shedding. There are various reasons for this paradox which are

---

59 See: Op. quoted previously.

60 Policy note on the Kaleta hydroelectric development on the Konkoure River, by Ousmane Tano Diallo, Consulting Electrical Engineer, energy specialist, September 2012.

61 See: (i) Guinea: Policy note on Electricity and Water, Emilio Sacerdoci, Consultant, World Bank, 21 May 2010; (ii) Report on Guinea's economic and social situation 2009-2011, Ministry of Planning, national Directorate of Planning, Conakry, November 2012.

due to the conditions in which independence of Guinea was reached, to the Guinean leaders' lack of vision, to misdirected energy policies and to the poor level of equipment of the sector, thus preventing EDG (Electricity of Guinea) to meet the increased demand of 7% per annum[62].

The deficit in the energy supply has serious consequences on the well-being of the people, trade, industry and SMEs/ SMIs which often rely on generators to operate. The operating and maintenance costs of these generators, together with other factors (the road density level in Guinea is the lowest of the sub-region, i.e. 2.8km/100km2 in 2010), lead to high costs in produced goods and services. The competitiveness of the Guinean economy is very low compared to that of other countries of the sub-region.

Furthermore, in spite of the great hydroelectric potential and the large quantity of fire-wood which amount to 85% of the total energy consumption of the country, Guinea's energy consumption per capita valued at 500 kep is one of the lowest of the sub-region. The contribution of energy and factories to the GDP is only 11.92%.

In the expectation of the improvement of access to electricity in the medium and long term, and in the context of energy development within a regional integration plan (Western African Power Pool-WAPP), the World Bank and other international financial organisations consider supporting Government's efforts to implement a strategy to expand hydroelectric production. The WAPP, financed by the World Bank, is conducting a

62 See: Assessment report of the rehabilitation and extension project of Conakry's electrical networks, Guinea, African Development Bank, July 2008.

study to define a strategy for the optimal hydroelectric development. The preliminary results of this study show special interest for Kaléta (under way), Souapiti, Fomi, Amaria, Morissanannko, Kassa and Gogoguezia.

However, if the hydroelectric energy sector was rationally exploited, it could be a powerful engine for economic growth in the country. In this respect, one only needs to look at the hydroelectric developments on the Konkouré River (Garafiri-Souapiti-Kaleta-Amaria) to assess what the hydroelectric potential of Guinea represents for the national economy.

Many surveys and studies have been conducted on the Konkouré River and the interest in this site goes back to the 1920s. As a matter of fact, according to a report updated in September 2012, an American mission carried out the first flow measurements on the Konkouré River, at Kaléma in particular[63]. Since then, many other studies have been undertaken by the Government, international Offices or Organisations, the latest one being an environmental and social impact study of Souapiti financed by the African Development Bank. According to a document by Consulting Engineer COB produced in January 2003, (i) the identified hydroelectric potential of Konkouré is in the order of 5 500 GWh/annum, of which some 85% is guaranteed; and (ii) the identified levels that can be developed on the three sites would give the following results: Garafiri (227/272 GWh/annum); Souapiti (2640/2825 GWh/annum);

[63] See: « Souapiti: un site prometteur pour l'industrialisation de la Guinée et l'intégration énergétique sous régionale ». Connaissance du potentiel hydroélectrique du fleuve Konkouré. A summary prepared by Ousmane Tanou Diallo, Consulting Electrical Engineer, specialist in energy.

Kaléta (980/1035 GWh/annum); and Amaria (1020/1435 GWh/annum). Only Garafiri is being exploited (although the building of this dam did not bring about the expected results), since Kaléta is still under construction. There remains thus a potential of 4193 GWh/annum to develop.

According to some projections, Souapity alone, in the production phase, could generate revenues amounting to US$302.89 million per year from 2018 to 2035[64]. Hydroelectricity is therefore a real gold mine for the Guinean economy, not only in terms of the increase of the capacity of energy production and exportation of the country, but also in terms of employment and stimulus given to the activities of SMEs/SMIs and mining industries.

However, the targets to be met in the Energy sector by 2015 seem unattainable since there is so much delay in the implementation of infrastructures. As a matter of fact, it is a pipe dream to believe that we will achieve an electrification rate of 65% (OMD) or 50% (CEDEAO) with 100% in urban areas and 36% in rural areas. On the other hand, we can achieve these targets by 2020 if we make, as of now, all the technical and financial provisions to develop the hydroelectric potential.

It is imperative to implement a sectorial strategy based on the following elements:

- State withdrawal from the sector by setting up a formal framework of Public-Private partnership (PPP).
- Promotion of a Mine-Energy-Industry synergy. With the development of the Konkouré complex

[64] See: Souapiti, op. already quoted

(Amaria-Souapiti-Kaléta), Guinea will be able to develop a heavy industry based on the production of aluminium and steel, instead of remaining an exporter of mining raw materials, as is currently the case.

- Control of energy consumption.

Guinea is certainly a country destined for hydroelectricity, even if the thermal sector is currently dominating with 68%. Finally, the aim must be to reach the right balance between (i) the large and micro-dams; and (ii) the thermal energy, hydroelectricity and renewable energies to give the country a regular and satisfactory electricity supply.

No development is possible without sufficient electricity. The progress made in other socio-economic sectors is subject to the availability of energy, especially the mining industry, the manufacturing industry, SMEs/SMIs, hospitals, telecommunications, etc.

The difficulties met by EDG in the supply are due to the following factors: (i) the State's arrears in the payment of its invoices; (ii) the State's insufficient support in rate adjustments and the introduction of reforms in the sector; and (iii) EDG's failure to make the essential adjustments, control costs, improve relations with the clients, reduce technical and commercial losses and combat fraud. Moreover, there is a need for the reliable supply and billing of electricity, if the upstream problems are resolved, especially the building of dams (Kaléta partially meets this need).

CHAPTER NINE

THIRD PILLAR: BETTER EXPLOITATION AND USE OF MINING RESOURCES

Transparency and political will are crucial for mining to have an impact on the economic and social development.

Guinea's mining wealth has been abundantly exploited and highlighted since colonial times. Guinea has been generously endowed by nature as a result of its hydrological, agricultural and mining potential (bauxite, iron, gold, diamonds, titanium, limestone, uranium, manganese, graphite, etc.).

The country has the world's largest reserves of bauxite put at 40 billion tons[65]. This figure could be further increased by 10 billion tons taking into account the bauxite areas with low alumina content in the North-east of Guinea (from Siguiri to Beyla). Thus, at a rate of 20 million tons of bauxite produced per year out of 100 million tons consumed in the world, it would ensure Guinea 2 500 years, i.e. 25 centuries of production.

As for iron, the South-East of Guinea has the largest and richest deposit in the world which is not yet exploit-

[65] See: Ibrahima Soumah, *Avenir de l'Industrie minière en Guinée*, Editions l'Harmattan, Paris, 2006.

ed. The centre-south area of the country also has a large iron deposit. The known reserves are estimated at 12 billion tons of high-grade iron (more than 60%).

As far as gold is concerned, the reserves are carefully estimated at several hundred tons. The north-east of the country is the epicentre of large gold deposits. The main producing regions are Dinguiraye, Kouroussa, Siguiri and Mandiana. The current annual production of gold is around 35 tons.

Finally, the diamond reserves are over 30 million carats. In 2012, production was around 333 000 carats. There are other minerals in Guinea's underground, in particular uranium in the Kissidougou region (Firawa), copper, lead, zinc, cobalt, limestone (40 million tons), nickel (75 million tons), graphite, etc. To these substances must be added building materials such as igneous rock (granite, syenite, dolerite, gabbros, etc.) which are present in most regions, and black sand minerals (ilmenite, rutile, zirconia, etc.)[66].

Since the country became independent in 1958, Guinea's economic growth comes essentially from mining, especially bauxite, the country being the first exporter of it in the world. As a matter of fact, the contribution of the mining sector of the GDP is around 15% (see Table 1). The mining contribution in the public revenues amounted in 2010 to US$210 million. Export taxes for diamond, gold and the leasing of infrastructures represent also a source of revenues for the Government. The lease of CBG infrastructures (Compagnie des Bauxites de Guinée) generates revenue of US$6.5 million per annum to the State.

---

[66] See: Guinea CPD, Sector profile Mining, document previously quoted.

According to the World Bank, the mining sector generates over 10 000 direct jobs. Moreover, over 200 000 operators are active in the artisanal mining of alluvial gold and diamonds[67].

During the same period, mining represented 28.0% to 31% of the income of the State Budget (see Table 1). Compared to the country's total exports, they amounted to 84.1%; 88.9% and 87.2%, in 2006, 2007 and 2008 respectively.

Table 1: Contribution of the mining sector to the Guinean economy from 2006 to 2011.

Year	2006	2007	2008	2009	2010	2011
Amount (in thousands of US$)	128 220	136 970	160 580	151 780	173 340	219 600
In public revenue %	31.51 %	24.4 %	24.1 %	21.9 %	26.2 %	28.60 %
Contribution to GDP	14.4 %	14.5 %	15.8 %	14.7 %	14.5 %	14.2 %

Source: Ministry of Economy and Finance, 2012.

In 40 years of operation, CBG has brought over US$4 billion to Guinea[68] for a corresponding production of 400 million tons of bauxite and for a global commer-

[67] See: Guinea CPD, Sector profile Mining, 2013, document presented at Abu Dhabi Forum.

[68] See: Ibrahima Soumah, *Avenir de l'industrie minière en Guinée*, Editions l'Harmattan, Paris, 2006. Table page XII.

cial value of US$15 billion. The same quantity of bauxite transformed into alumina amounts to US$80 billion, and in aluminium metal to US$200 billion. These processings which yield more money are industrial and not simply mining operations.

Unfortunately, Guinea is at one end of the chain and cannot at this level benefit from the added values obtained from the processing of bauxite into alumina, and that of alumina into aluminium. If bauxite was processed in Guinea, the following results could be obtained: two tons of processed bauxite yield one ton of alumina. Yet, the added value is multiplied by ten, since one ton of bauxite can be sold for US$30/t, while one ton of alumina can be sold for US$300. Two tons of processed alumina yield one ton of aluminium for a value multiplied by seven, and the price of one ton of aluminium can amount to US$2000[69].

In addition to direct added values coming from local processing, the additional effects of this characterisation of the Guinean mining industry are even more important: creation of subcontracting SME/SMIs essential for the balanced functioning of bauxite, alumina and aluminium production units. Each processing stage will require qualified and competent technicians and executives who will have to be trained.

On the other hand, if Guinea had taken better advantage of the exportation of this ore, and if it had made better use of the revenues from the exportation of the ores, it would certainly be among middle-income or emerging countries.

---

[69] On 1/09/2014, the spot sales price of aluminium was US$2114.00/ton. And the sales price three months later was US$2099/t.

Since the arrival a few years ago of *major* companies in our country (BHP Billiton, Rio Tinto, Vale, etc.), the development prospects of extractive industries have been good and should lead the mining sector to be a driving force of economic growth. Two large societies are currently operating in the gold mines (the Société minière de Dinguiraye (SMD- Russian) and la Société Aurifère de Guinée (SAG of Anglo-Gold Ashanti). Besides these companies, many artisanal gold and diamond miners operate in the country. Concerning Bauxite and alumina, there are three active companies, namely the Compagnie des bauxites de Guinée (CBG), the Compagnie des bauxites de Kindia (CBK) and Alumina Company of Guinea – ACG-Rusal. Other companies are waiting in the wings to mine iron and bauxite, in particular Rio Tinto/SIMFER, China Power Investment, Vale/BSGR, Bellezone, etc. Investments are anticipated at billions of US$. Just for iron, investments in the order of 18 billion are expected for an annual exportation of 250 million tons of iron (World Bank, 2012).

If these projects materialise, there could be a double-digit GDP growth before 2020. Thus Guinea could become a medium-income country and join the path of emerging African countries. However, the gap must be rapidly bridged between investments intentions and real investments. It will depend on the incentives the Government will offer to the Majors through a revised mining Code. What is important in mining is less the necessary participation of the State to the capital of mining companies than the multiplier effects of investments at the economic, financial and agricultural level, and the strengthening of human and institutional capacities.

Mining operations first benefit mining companies and the State; the latter will have the responsibility of benefitting the people, in particular through infrastructure projects. The transmission mechanisms of these beneficial effects are biased, while the development of agriculture has a direct effect on the standard of living of the farmers, and thus contributes more significantly to the reduction of poverty. Providing food and income to the farmers will improve their standard of living (better housing, health insurance, means of transport through buying bicycles and motorbikes, etc.)

Therefore, it is necessary to diversify the economy by supporting the agricultural sector as mentioned above and by taking advantage of the huge hydroelectric potential of the country. The energetic deficit is a constraint on the development of mining industries.

Developing these three pillars of Guinea's Transformation Strategy (agriculture, energy and mining) will result in multiplier effects on other sectors. All of them generate jobs and income. The taxation of natural resources provides much income to the State. Yet, agriculture and cattle-breeding are not subject to taxation. The increase in State revenues should contribute much to financing the social sectors, especially health and education. The government must not forget that "it is necessary to encourage agricultural activities when a mine is developing, to feed the hundred and even thousands of workers working there"[70]. The mining

[70] See: La Guinée, sa « terre »: potentiels minier et agricole et son peuple: potentiel humain, by M. Denis Thirouin, mining expert, Secretary general of the Mifergui-Nimba company.

potential does not feed anyone. As Denis Thirouin said, the Guinean political class should understand that, "*in spite of the wealth and potential of the country, often referred to as a high quality 'geological scandal', no factory in the world ended production because of a lack*

CHAPTER TEN

FOURTH PILLAR:
IMPROVEMENT OF GOVERNANCE AND STRENGTHENING OF CAPACITIES

The consolidation of democracy and the rule of law will in turn strengthen good governance

The term Good governance has been overused in Africa. All the countries on the continent talk about it and the governments are committed to implementing it. Senegal has even created a Ministry responsible for promoting good governance; Burkina Faso has established a permanent Secretariat of national policy of good governance; and Guinea has a Ministry of Human Rights and public Liberties.

Yet few countries apply all its basic principles, namely: citizen participation to decision-making, primacy of law, transparency, equity, efficiency, responsibility and respect of international, regional and sub-regional commitments.

Good governance is synonymous with a better distribution of the wealth of a country and better ways of governing and managing the country.

"*Good governance would guarantee better economic*

---

of raw materials from Guinea, whether for aluminium or steel production, Guinea's two poles of excellence".

performances. Good governance implies the existence of adequate institutional, human and material capacities, as well as strong and well-balanced actors (public administration, executive, legislative and judicial powers, civil society)"[71] .

Gogue goes on to say that: "*The consolidation of democracy in African countries requires an improvement of the living conditions of the people. This condition can only be fulfilled if the governments manage to improve the economic performance of their countries; which in turn requires good governance. The analysis shows that in spite of reforms in the public service, progress in the education system, and institutional strengthening programmes implemented in many countries, the current institutional and human capacities of African countries and the efficiency of public administration are still poor. The other actors of governance who must act as a counterweight to the executive are in most cases not able to play their part efficiently. The strengthening of institutional and human capacities of the different actors of governance is a priority to guarantee the consolidation of good governance practice in African countries* ".

As for Guinea, it has made the first step towards establishing the conditions for good governance by establishing republican institutions since 2010, a democratically elected President for the first time in the country's history, a national Assembly and a Supreme

---

[71] See: Gouvernance en Afrique: Etat des lieux, in Etudes et Recherches économiques No 67, African Development Bank, by Tchaboure Aimé Gogue, Faculté des Sciences économiques et Sciences de Gestion (FASEG), Université de Lome.

Court. All these institutions must strive to meet the needs of the Guinean people in matters of Law.

The adhesion of Guinea, a mining country, to the ITIE (Initiative of Transparency in the Mining Industries) is a step towards the strengthening of transparency in the management of mining resources, ITIE being a good instrument for promoting good governance.

The press is free and speaks unimpeded on issues of national interest. There are even satirical weekly papers that do not refrain from deriding the government. However, civil society organisations do not yet have an influence on political and economic decisions to represent, together with the media, a true counter force, as in established democratic countries.

Opposition parties speak and meet freely to state their case on issues that are vital for the country's future. However, often violent demonstrations are the result of disagreements between the government and the opposition parties on electoral timetables.

Measures were taken to create an environment favourable for the private sector: increasing the energy supply, establishing a single desk for start-up formalities, reducing the time required to obtain building permits, etc. Yet, there is a need for impartial justice to reassure citizens and investors, even if the current reforms of the justice system (establishment of the Supreme Judicial Council) are increasingly moving along these lines.

In public administration, human, material, technical and financial means have been put in place to better meet citizens' needs, yet ordinary citizens still find it difficult to obtain the desired services, without having to take multiple steps themselves to follow a dossier through the administrative route, wasting time, energy and sometimes their own money. The establishment in the Ministry of Justice of the National Directorate of access to Rights and Justice should remedy this situation.

Financial resources have been mobilised, but their investment into public interest projects often sustains many losses which diminish their impact on the improvement of people's living conditions.

Decentralisation which is still incomplete, negatively affects grass-root accountability and participation. It is an impediment to local good governance.

It is necessary to put safeguards in place to avoid embezzlements, by making justice impartial and accessible to all citizens, including the most vulnerable ones. Without corruption-free justice, investors, whether Guinean or foreign, will lack confidence. In general, direct foreign investments look for countries with strong institutions, impartial laws and optimal transparent conditions.

Finally, one must keep in mind that ethics and technical competence must be taken into account when promoting cadres to the highest positions of the State[72]. The appointment of civil servants with doubtful integrity gives the youth a bad image of public administration. They might reduce their efforts in school, convinced that excellence does not pay, since other more subjective criteria are taken into account in the appointment and promotion of employees.

Chapter 2 explains sufficiently the conditions and the beneficial effects of good governance in a country. The main lesson to remember is that more power must be

---

[72] See: Mamadi Camara, Où va la Guinée? Editions l'Harmattan, Paris, 2010, page l'Art des nominations.

given to institutions in order to strengthen the rule of law.

It must also be remembered that without good governance, the benefits obtained under the first three pillars will be limited and their positive effects on the people and the economic development will be poor.

Finally, as a conclusion for the chapters dealing with the pillars of the development strategy, we must stress the fact that all public and private life actors must have a development mentality without which the implementation of development programmes and projects of the country will encounter obstacles that will have a negative effect on expected results.

CHAPTER ELEVEN

THE EXAMPLE OF CAPE VERDE

All observers are impressed by the progress made by men and women in this country handicapped by its geography. From very little, they achieved much in a relatively short time.

There is a wide range of countries in Africa, ranging from fragile states, post-conflict states, less advanced countries to medium income countries. Yet, never has a country with so few natural resources and so little land suitable for agriculture made such progress. This small insular country can serve as an inspiration for other African countries.

History and geography

Cape Verde is a small insular country consisting of 10 islands scattered[73] in the Atlantic Ocean, off the coasts of Senegal, Gambia and Mauritania. This fragmented country with an area of 4033 km² was discovered in 1460 by the Portuguese. But, another version of the country's history mentions the presence of Senega-

[73] See: Michel Lesourd, Insularism and Development in the Republic of Cape Verde, Laboratory for arid region studies, University of Rouen, February 1994.

lese, Arab and Greek fishermen before the arrival of the Portuguese.

At times a fairly flourishing trading post between Portugal and West Africa, transit point in the triangular slave trade between Europe, Africa and America, the islands become gradually settled depending on the potential of each island. Today, a people of mixed race between Europeans and descendants of African slaves, represent 80% of the total population.

All the islands of the archipelago are of volcanic origin (Santiago, Boa Vista, Fogo, Sao Tiago, Maio, Sal, Sao Nicolao, Santa Luzia, Sao Vicente and Santo Antao). They have a very high relief with volcanic ash covering the ground and little vegetation. Fogo island has the highest summit (2829m) in the country, called Pico do Fogo which had a lava flow in 1995. The climate causes frequent droughts and the islands are often struck with sand storms coming from the Sahara. Most of the 9 inhabited islands have a Sahelian hilly landscape with a desert-type vegetation. This arid land is largely unsuitable for agriculture and the rainfall is poor (an average of 250 mm of rain per annum, while Guinea gets an average of 4000 mm in the Conakry region).

Liberation struggle and demographic process under way

The Portuguese colonisation lasted 600 years. In 1956 a liberation movement was created outside the archipelago, in Guinea Bissau with the creation of the PAIGC, African party for the Independence of Guinea-Bissau and Cape Verde islands, by a Cape verdant agricultural engineer, Amilcar Cabral and his companions, as well as his brother Luis Cabral and Aristide Pereira.

An armed struggle conducted essentially in Guinea-Bissau, opposed the PAIGC to Portugal until 1974, when Antonio Salazar was deposed by Spinola, paving the way for negotiations with the PAIGC which led to the independence of Guinea-Bissau in October 1974 with Luis Cabral as the first President. A few months later, on 5 July 1975, Cape Verde also achieved international sovereignty with Aristide Pereira as its first President.

After the coup d'état of 1980 in which Joao Bernardo Vieira, a former freedom fighter of Guinea-Bissau, overthrew Luis Cabral, the archipelago seceded from Guinea-Bissau and created the PAICV, the African Party for the Independence of Cape Verde. The unitary state came to an end and Cape Verde created its own national sovereignty symbols: flag, national anthem, coat of arms, etc.

In 1990, following the fall of the Berlin Wall and the Soviet bloc, Cape Verde established a multiparty system. There are 8 parties altogether, the main three being the PAICV, the Movement for Democracy (MpD) and UCID (Independent and

Democratic Cape Verdean Union or UCID) who have MPs in the national Assembly. In 1991, the first multiparty elections would bring the MpD to power. The government started a vast privatisation programme which gave the impression that it was selling the country's wealth to Portugal, with disastrous social consequences. The MpD paid the consequences of the privatisations which had a high social cost, and the PAICV came back to power during the presidential elections of 1996.

Since 1991, four presidential elections have taken place, with the two larger parties, namely the MpD and the PAICV, alternating rule. In the current legislature since 2012, there is a peaceful cohabitation with a President from the MpD and the Prime Minister from the PAICV, the winner of legislative elections. These democratic practices worthy of the old western democracies, show the degree of maturity reached by the country in political governance, and make of Cape Verde a model country in terms of democracy.

The former President of the Republic, Pedro Pires, received the Mo Ibrahim prize, awarded to African leaders who best achieved good governance. Pires is considered as one of the main architects of economic and social progress of Cape Verde. Under his presidency, the UN awarded his country, by a resolution in 2008, the status of middle-income country. After two mandates he left office in 2011, after organising presidential elections which his own party lost.

The keys to success

Four main factors are responsible for Cape Verde's economic and social performances: the strengthening of human capital, good economic and financial governance, socio-political stability and soundness of institutions, and transfer of revenues from the Diaspora and international aid. These outstanding performances are supported by reforms and policies of development and fight against poverty.

The authorities, aware of their country's lack of natural resources, have invested massively in the Education sector. The results obtained are striking: the school enrolment rate is over 90%; the adult literacy rate is one of the highest in Africa (84.8%), i.e. a higher rate than the average for Sub-Saharan Africa (61.6%). Gender parity is nearly reached in primary education: in 2009/2010, there were 48% girls versus 52% boys. In secondary education, there are more girls than boys (54% versus 42%). In addition to this progress, the elite receive special training that meets the requirements of modem life. Most of the executives who hold managerial positions in public administration can speak not only Portuguese but also English and/or French.

The second success factor is good economic and financial governance. In the management of public finance, the country has undertaken extensive reforms which reduced corruption and provided transparency. This is the main reason for the high scores of the country in the international indicators of good governance. Cape Verde ranks (i) 2nd among the 53 countries of Sub-Saharan Africa in the 2011 Mo Ibrahim index of African governance; (ii) it ranks 45th out of 178 countries in the 2010 corruption perception index of Transparency International, i.e. the 3rd best performance in this part of Africa. The establishment of the Maison du Citoyen (Citizen House) which has branches in the country and an online site, enables all Cape Verdeans to have access to information on the performance of public administration, (particularly budgetary figures), its management and specific formalities (the creation of firms, for instance).

The third factor concerns socio-political stability and soundness of institutions. Since the country became independent in 1975, the alternation in government of the two largest parties takes place smoothly and in a civilised manner. There were even periods of cohabitation at the state helm, as is the case since the last presidential elections held on 7 August 2011 with a second round on 21 August 2011 which led to the election of the MpD candidate, Jorge Carlos FONSECA as President of the Republic with 53.4% against the PAICV candidate, Manuel Inocienco SOUSA, with 46.6% of the votes. However, the legislative elections of 6 February 2011 ensured the victory of the PAICV, opening the way to a cohabitation in the running of public affairs. The fourth factor is the corollary of these three factors which guarantee that they are implemented properly, namely international aid and remittances from the Diaspora. They are the fourth key of the socio-economic performances of Cape Verde. The remittances from the 700 000 Cape Verdeans living abroad (United States, Portugal, France, and the Netherlands) represent close to 10% of the GDP each year.

The savings transferred by the Diaspora are a windfall for the country: US$145 million in 2009, i.e. 9.1% of the GDP and US$292.33 per capita. Public development aid amounted to US$196 million in 2009, i.e. 9.12% of the GDP and US$395.16% per capita. FDIs amounted to 9.3 billion Cape Verdean escudos (CVE)[74] in 2010 and decreased by one third, 6.1 billion CVE[75] in 2011. Moreover, Cape Verde is an important recipient of the Millennium Challenge Corporation's financial resources. Finally, since 25 March 2011, the country harbours the Maritime Security Operation Centre (COSMAR), financed with US$3 million by the American funds of the USAFRICOM project. The main bilateral and multilateral donors are: Portugal, the United States, Luxemburg, the Netherlands, Austria, the Euro-

---

[74] The escudo, Cape Verde currency, has been linked to the euro since 1999. 1 Euro= 110 Cape Verdean escudos.

[75] See : Economic perspectives for Africa in 2012, Cape verde Note.

pean Union, the World Bank and the African Development Bank.

On the basis of these four factors, the Government has started the economic and social development of the country. To this end, it has set up a long-term vision document named Economic Transformation Strategy (STE) and a Growth and Poverty Reduction Strategy Paper (DSCRP) to implement the STE development objectives on the basis of 4 year cycles.

In the absence of natural resources, Cape Verde focused its development on the services which represented 80% of the GDP in 2010. Over the past decade, the country focused on the development of tourism which dominates the service sector or tertiary sector (80%) and contributes 26% to the GDP. The greatest part of foreign direct investments go to tourism, fostering the activities in the construction sector (buildings and public works) and real estate.

Cape Verde was removed from the list of least developed countries (PMA) in January 2008, due to the economic transformation strategy defined by the government. Since 1997, the government has implemented poverty reduction strategies which will become growth and poverty reduction strategies in 2000. In May 2008, the authorities formulated the second Growth and Poverty Reduction Strategy Paper (DSCRP-II) with a participative approach including all the country's stakeholders. The DSCRP-II is based on the following main objectives: reduce unemployment to less than 10%, reach an accelerated real economic growth rate higher than 10% and reduce poverty by half. Cape Verde is one of the rare African countries which are in a good position to reach all the Millennium development objectives (OMD) by 2015. The economic growth rates achieved at the beginning of the millennium contributed to the reduction of poverty. The proportion of the people living below the poverty line decreased from 49% in 1988-89, to 37% in 2001-2002 and to 27% in 2007[76].

In the last ten years (2002-2012), the country achieved an average growth of 6.1%, with a peak of 10.8% in 2006. However, due to the international financial crisis and the debt crisis in Europe (the escudo has been pegged to the euro since 1999), the economic growth has slowed down, settling at 3.6% in 2006, before jumping to 5.4% in 2010 and 5% in 2011. The inflation that had reached 6.8% in 2008 decreased to 2.1% in 2010 and should remain low in the next few years. The economy relies on the service sector which represents 80% of the GDP with tourism as the driver of the economy. Agriculture as a whole contributes only 11% to the GDP and industry and energy 9%. Exports remain marginal, as the country only exports fish and textile. Lacking natural resources and farming land, the country focuses on the development of services which attract many direct foreign investments. "*These progresses made it possible for Cape Verde to go in 2008 from the least developed countries category (PMA) to that of the middle-income countries (PRI) and to be classified among the first African countries regarding governance* "[77].

In spite of this economic and social progress, Cape Verde is facing important challenges, especially unemployment which affected 10.7% of the population in

---

[76] See: Cape Verde: country file, September 2009, World Bank

[77] See: Cape Verde: Assessment of the Bank assistance 1996-2007, Department of operations evaluation (OPEV), 15 October 2009, African Development Bank group.

2010, against 13.1% in 2009. Unemployment is higher among the youth (the young people of 15-24 constitute 50% of the active population), women and the rural population. In 2010, 20.1% of the youth were unemployed[78] .

Main lessons

In less than 20 years (1991-2008), Cape Verde went from the least developed countries category (PMA) to that of the middle-income countries (PRI) on the United Nations scale. The geographic handicaps dictated the way to follow to the leaders of the country to ensure the economic and social development of Cape Verde, relying on four main factors: tourism, transfer of revenues from the Diaspora, external aid and political, economic and financial governance.

Thus, "*strong economic growth and decrease in poverty can be achieved with a combination of adequate reform policies, good governance, development focused on reducing poverty, and the increased mobilisation of external resources* "[79].

Cape Verde's strong economic development in the last ten years shows that a country with no natural resources can get out of the poverty trap by turning a geographic handicap into an advantage, simply through the virtues of good governance. As a matter of fact, good governance in public affairs brings about multiplier effects on the mobilisation of internal and external resources which will help finance the economic

[78] See: Economic perspectives for Africa in 2012, Cape Verde Note.
[79] See: Cape Verde: Assessment of bank assistance 1996-2007, document already quoted.

programmes of the government. In fact, good governance catalyses the mobilisation of the State's financial resources. Political and economic stability attracts foreign investments (FDIs) and public development aid, and transfers of revenues from citizens residing abroad. It also attracts foreign tourists who during their stay spend money to pay their hotel bills and to buy souvenirs. This creates the need for hotel infrastructures which stimulates activities in the construction sector. Finally, the transmission mechanisms of this virtuous circle make it possible to pass on the effects of good governance to all sectors of the national economy.

If a disadvantaged country can achieve wonders, why not a country generously endowed by nature? What is lacking in countries rich in natural resources (petroleum, mines, agriculture, etc.), is organisation and method, and a strong sense of State interest, patriotism and the meaning of history. All these ingredients can be found in good governance. In fact, by elaborating and applying rigorously a code of good conduct in the management of public affairs, the leaders of a country have the means to exploit national resources in the best interest of the populations. These serious internal shortcomings have also been encouraged or allowed by the corruptive practices of many foreign companies.

In applying the principles of good governance as in Cape Verde, the countries with abundant natural resources can obtain even better results in a shorter time, since nature "facilitates" their social and economic development objectives.

CHAPTER TWELVE

THE EXAMPLE OF GHANA

Ghana, a former British colony that became independent on 6 March 1957, abandoned its former colonial name (Gold Coast, due to its many gold mines exploited by British settlers) for that of Ghana to pay tribute to the ancient empire of Ghana. It is the first British colony in Africa that achieved independence (after Liberia that became independent in 1847) under the leadership of the *Osagyefo*, Dr. Kwame N'Krumah who became the first Prime Minister in 1957 and the first President on 1 July 1960 when the country became a Republic. N'Krumah became a great Pan-Africanist and was one of the founding fathers of the Organisation of African Unity. Ghana would be followed on the road of independence in 1958 by Guinea with which it would develop close political cooperation relations.

Ghana is situated in West Africa on the Gulf of Guinea. It has an area of 239 360km² with a coast line of 539km and borders with Côte d'Ivoire in the west, Burkina Faso in the north and Togo in the east. In 2013 its population was estimated at 25 million inhabitants.

Ghana has abundant natural wealth, including agricultural products such as cocoa, wood, coffee, mahogany, and pineapple which are exported. Ghana is the second biggest exporter of cocoa with a production of 1 million tons in 2010-2011, Côte d'Ivoire being the first world producer with 1.4 million (official Ivorian sources). In fact, 4 African countries supply 72% of the world production of coffee beans (Côte d'Ivoire, Ghana, Nigeria and Cameroon)[80]. According to Professor I.Y. Opokou, deputy executive director of the *Coconut Research Institute of Ghana*, based in Accra, cocoa cultivation contributes 30% of the GDP and employs 600 000 farmers. Moreover, the forest is one of the country's assets. According to the Forest Commission of Ghana, wood and forest products exports amounted to 251 364m³ in 2012[81].

It has a variety of mineral wealth, especially gold, the country being the 8th world producer of gold and the 2nd in the continent after South Africa (Ghana's gold production was 100 tons in 2011)[82], diamonds, manganese and bauxite, and recently petroleum and gaz. Ghana ranks third in terms of oil reserves in Sub-Saharan Africa, far behind Nigeria and Angola. As a matter of fact, Ghana's oil reserves amount to about 490 million barrels for 37 200 million barrels for Nigeria and 9 500 for Angola. In 2011, production came to 80 000 barrels per day for 2 million barrels per day on average for Nigeria[83].

Yet, how did a country, embroiled in recurring upheavals and coups d'états and attempted coup d'états in

---

[80] See: Official paper of the Conference of member countries of the Alliance of cocoa-producing countries (copal), which met at Yaounde, Cameroon, on 8-12 October 2012 for their 75th general assembly.
[81] See: Agence Ecofin Agro of 16 April 2013.
[82] See: Laurent Curau, Fondateur@cafedela brousse.com, on 19 November 2012, from the publications of the World Gold Council.
[83] See: Ghana: strategy paper for country 2012-2016, African development Bank, ORWA, 2012.

the first two decades of its independence, managed to recover and become a model of good political, economic and financial governance.

Keys to success

Ghana has a relative and encouraging success story which deserves special attention from which many lessons can be learned in terms of political and economic governance.

First key: a broad vision of democracy and ethical advances prevailed

Ghana has had a multiparty system since the 1950s, which was interrupted in 1960 by the first President of the country, *Osagyefo* Kwame N'Krumah who introduced the one party state. After the 1966 coup d'état which toppled N'Krumah, the periods of civil rule were constantly interrupted by military dictatorships. In 15 years, from 1966 to 1981, the political life has been marked by four coups d'état and three attempted coups in 1982, 1983 and 1984. This political instability has had disastrous consequences on the Ghanaian economy. As a matter of fact, the level of the real GDP per capita had decreased by 40% at the beginning of 1983, and the national currency has weakened considerably.

However, the military dictatorship enabled Jerry Rawlings to impose a code of conduct for financial management and a greater respect for public assets, by force. By punishing sometimes close relatives, Rawlings developed a sense of moral responsibility and the principle of responsibility and honesty in public life[84]. On this ethical foundation he gradually strengthened democracy, the institutions and the rule of law.

The country only stabilised on 28 April 1992 with the adoption of a new Constitution establishing multiparty, liberalism and a balance of power with the separation of the executive, legislature and judiciary. Jerry Rawlings' election on 3 November 1992 and the proclamation of the 4th Republic on 7 January 1993 mark the beginning of the strengthening of institutions in Ghana's political governance. With each general election (there have been 6 since 1992), the country showed increasing democratic maturity with high levels of participation, as was the case with the presidential elections of December 2012 (80.1 %). Thus, Ghana became the most stable and most prosperous country in West Africa[85].

Political life is dominated by two large parties: the *New Patriotic Party* (NPP) and the *National Democratic Congress* (NDC). Opposition parties often adopt constructive positions and the same objectives as the governing party. Only the paths that lead to it differ. For instance, during the electoral campaign for the 2012 presidential elections, the governing NDC and the NPP had both put the development of human resources through the health insurance for all Ghanaians, at the centre of their programme, on the one hand, and, the strengthening of basic education, on the other hand. At the education level, only the approach differed. While the former wanted to get there by building school infra-

---

[84] See: Political history, extracted from the booklet "Ghana - a brief guide", a publication from the Ghana Information Services Department 1994.

[85] See: Political History, op. already quoted.

structures, training and qualifying teachers, and eventually free education, the latter was proposing an immediate free primary and secondary education.

It should be noted that since its independence, and even during the periods of political insatiability, there was always much emphasis on education, so much so that it was made compulsory from the 1961 Constitution (The Education Act of 1961) to this day with the Free Compulsory Universal basic Education -FCUBE- (1992 Constitution). Surely this explains in part the remarkable evolution of the country's political culture, making it an example in the sub-region, in terms of the strength of its political institutions.

At each step in the strengthening of democracy, the leaders have shown a great political maturity. Contesting the results of the 2012 election, the NPP filed an annulment appeal before the Supreme Court, but accepted its judgment which confirmed its defeat, without street demonstrations.

Thus, the institutions operate satisfactorily, the executive being controlled by the legislative, the organisations of civil society and the press which has developed considerably in recent years. According to Dr. Gyimah-Boadi, Director of the *Ghana Centre for Democratic Development* (CDD): "Twenty years ago press freedom was actively repressed. Today, we have over 140 commercial radio stations and some 50 private television channels, and a huge number of newspapers and magazines. Each morning, some or other minister must come and explain his policy on a radio programme. In the old days, this was unthinkable”. This great freedom of expression was established by the *Freedom of Information Bill* (access to information bill) and the *Whistle Blowers Bill* (whistle blowers protection bill) submitted to the Government in 2004.

In terms of the strengthening of democracy and political stability, Ghana's performances are the base on which the country established its economic expansion.

Thus, from the middle of the 1980s, a sustained recovery was initiated and increased in the following years[86].

Second key: properly implemented economic policies

There are three benchmarks in Ghana's economic evolution: the 1960-1964 period showing a strong economic growth boosted by an industrialisation process to replace the importation of goods and services.

The 1965-1983 period was followed by political instability with the coup d'état in 1966 which toppled Kwame N'Krumah. The economic policies became inconsistent and a price and exchange control was established.

The 1983-2000 period saw the launching of a vast economic recovery to reduce State control with no sharing in the economy and the re-establishment of macro-economic stability. The strict implementation of this programme made it possible to reduce macro-economic imbalance and inflation. Result: the GDP growth rate reached an average of 4.5% between 1983 and 2000 and went up to 5.5% for the 200-2005 period. In 2006 there was a growth of 6.2%[87]. From this time onwards Ghana

---

[86] See: Markus Eberhardt and Francis Teal, "Ghana and Côte d'Ivoire: an inversion of the parts", in International Development policy, Revue international de politique de développement, January 20 I 0.

[87] See: Ghana, economic perspectives in Africa, BAfD/OCDE 2007.

was known as the "IMF good performer", because of the rigorous manner in which the country applied its economic and financial reform programmes with the support of the Brenton-Woods Institutions.

However, since the deterioration of the economic and financial situation in 2001, the Government developed its first poverty reducing strategy (GPRS I) in 2003, which was followed by a second document named Growth and Poverty Reducing Strategy of Ghana (GPRS II) for the 2006-2009 period. These reforms supported by donors made it possible to reach GDP growth rates never seen in previous periods with an average of 6% from 2004 to 2006. Meanwhile, in mid-2004, the country reached the completion point under the HIPC initiative, with a huge reduction of its debt. Moreover, the MDRI (Multilateral Debt Relief Initiative), added to the HIPCI, helping it to strengthen the establishment of its poverty reduction strategy. And the Ghana Living Standards Survey (GLSS-5) in 2006 provided convincing results: the poverty rate has dropped from 52% in 1992 to 39.5% in 1998 and to 28.5% in 2006. Although there are differences in the distribution of these percentages, they are a proof of the country's important progress. With these results, Ghana should reach the number I objective of the MDGs, namely the elimination of extreme poverty by 2015.

From the mid-80s, the country began a sustained economic recovery with an increase in the GDP growth rate. Since 1983, the average GDP growth rate has been increasing notably; it went from 4.5% from 1983 to 2000, to 5.5% for the 2000-2005 period. In 2006 there was a growth of 6.2%. From 2007, the country registered very high growth rates, due to the discovery of large offshore oil deposits in the south-west region of the country. The oil and gas production started in 2010.

This tendency prevailed with a slump in 2009 (4.7%) due to the international financial crisis, and a peak in 2011 (14.4%) following the start of oil production in 2010. The GDP growth rate remained at that level in 2012 with 7.1% and should reach 8% in 2013 and 8.7% in 2014[88]. "Thus in 2011, Ghana is the country with the highest economic growth in the world. In this year the GDP has vastly increased: by as much as 17%. Thus, since the 2000s, Ghana has the highest national GDP growth rate together with China and Cambodia. They are the only ones to go over 10% of annual growth in 2005."

The dynamics of this growth can be explained by the policy of economic diversification. As a matter of fact, instead of counting only on a single raw material or economic sector, the Ghanaian economy relies on cocoa and gold production, mining, the IT sector and the impulse brought about by oil exports since 2011[89]. In 2010-2011, Ghana produced 1 million tons of cocoa against 650 000 tons the previous year, and 100 tons of gold. Ghana has relied on the agricultural sector as the main pillar of its economic and social development, even if its services and oil contribute largely to the GDP. The part of agriculture in the GDP is around 35%.

[88] See: Economic Perspectives in Africa 2014, West Africa, Ghana, last update 06/09/2013.

[89] See: Ghana, Africa's rising star, in African Business, No 395 March 2013.

In 2011, cocoa brought a revenue of US$1.9 billion, 7% of the GDP (or 20% of the agricultural GDP)[90].

Access to electricity is 55%, i.e. the highest level in sub-Saharan Africa, except for South Africa (World Bank, August 2008).

Third key: political and social stability

Contrary to most West African countries, especially Liberia, Sierra Leone, Côte d'Ivoire and Nigeria, Ghana has not experienced intercommunity conflicts and civil wars in the last two decades. Therefore, the country has become more attractive for foreign investments. Moreover, the economic management in accordance with good governance criteria increases the confidence foreign countries have in the country. Thus, the limited attractiveness of other leading countries of the West African sub region, like Côte d'Ivoire and Nigeria (affected by conflicts linked to Islamism and insecurity), discourages investments and encourages foreign investors to invest their capital in rising powers like Ghana where democracy has made remarkable progress.

With the December 2012 elections, Ghana implemented its sixth constitutional political transition since the establishment of the 4th Republic in 1992, and shown a singular stability in a sub-region with many factors of instability.

In the last 20 years Ghana has had six peaceful and successful elections, with three alternations between the two largest parties of the country. This is proof that the

[90] See: Ghana: country strategy paper 2012-2016. Country Department, western region, 2012.

foundations of democracy are well-rooted in political life[91].

Fourth key: capital inflow

Due to Ghana's great attractiveness, foreign direct investments (FDIs) have been very high in recent years. According to estimates from the Ghana Investment Promotion Centre (GIPC), FDIs amounted to US$4.97 billion in the first three quarters of 2012. The mining sector, mainly gold, and oil exploration constitute the main sectors which attract FDIs. According to the UN report on investment in the world in 2011 of the UN Conference on Trade and Development (UNCTAD) Ghana was the 7th FDI beneficiary in Africa and the 3rd in Sub-Saharan Africa in 2010. According to the same report, the FDIs amounted to US$2.5 billion in 2010 against US$1.7 billion in 2009[92].

The countries investing the most in Ghana are: China, India, the United Kingdom, Lebanon and Nigeria. Thus, in 2012, China financed the greatest number of projects in Ghana while Lebanon was the first foreign investor in terms of the volume of investments. Moreover, Ghana is one of the greatest beneficiaries of official development assistance (ODA)[93].

In addition to these direct investments, Ghanaians abroad transfer a large part of their revenues to the

---

91 See: Ghana, Africa's rising star, in African business, No 395 March 2013

92 See: Ghana: country strategy paper 2012-2016. African Development Bank, 2012

93 See: Economic perspectives in Africa 2014, West Africa, Ghana, last update 06/09/2013.

country. According to an attaché from Ghana's High Commissariat in London, Ghanaians abroad send US$350-450 billion each year to their country[94]. These amounts increased in 2012, when Ghanaians from the Diaspora sent from US$2 to US$4 billion, according to estimates. According to the Bank of Ghana, the flow of transfers amounted to US$1.6 billion in 2009 and to US$2.12 billion in 2010[95].

According to the World Bank, Ghana's GDP represented 10.3% of West-Africa's GDP in 2009, thus ranking before Côte d'Ivoire (7.5%) and Senegal (4.7%) and after Nigeria (63.5%).

The four above-mentioned ingredients enabled Ghana to have a sustained economic growth and to join the lower middle-income countries in 2010. Thus, according to the IMF, the per capita income reached US$16.22 in 2012[96]. The economic prospects are promising with a growth rate estimated at 8.0% in 2013 and 8.7% in 2014. This growth will be pulled along by the gas and oil, agriculture and mines. When the oil production will reach its cruising speed (an estimated 250 000 barrel/day by 2013) the annual income from petroleum should be around US$1-2 billion.

In the last thirty years, Ghana achieved two major goals: the establishment and strengthening of republican

---

[94] See: the African Diaspora: Pan-Africanism or village solidarity? Paper presented at the third African Development Forum (ADF III), "Defining the priorities of regional Integration", UN Conference Centre, Addis Abeba (Ethiopia) , 3 – 8 March 2002; by Chukwu-emeka Chikezie, AFFORD.

[95] See box 2: Part of remittances by migrant workers in the Ghanaian economy, in Ghana: Country strategy paper 2012-2016, African Development Bank, 2012.

[96] See: IMF, *World Economic Outlook*, 2013.

institutions, on the one hand, and sustained growth, on the other hand. Parallelism between institutional and economic development is quite rare in Africa. Thus, in Côte d'Ivoire, the serious shortcomings of democracy and the weakness of institutions have led to the first coup d'état in 1999, to civil war and ethnic conflicts. Yet, "between 1960 and 1980, Côte d'Ivoire enjoyed an almost continuous growth so that, in 1980, its real Growth Domestic Product (GDP) per capita was two times higher than in the 1960s"[97].

In spite of its good performances, Ghana is still facing major challenges, including a high inflation rate (10% in 2012), a high incidence of poverty in the three northern regions, a budget deficit, a wage bill in the public service difficult to control, and a relatively poor productivity compared to other countries such as Kenya, Egypt, Mozambique, Malaysia or Thailand[98]. Ghana must also deal with the deterioration of the corruption perception in civil life, the limited access to drinking water (46% of the population had drinking water in 2005) and sanitation.

---

[97] See: Ghana and Côte d'Ivoire: an inversion of roles, *International development policy*/Revue internationale de la politique de developpement (online), 24 January 2014, by Markus Ehrhardt and Francis Teal, both researchers at Oxford University.

[98] See: Iza Lejarraga, the purring tiger or the mewing cat: diagnostic study of growth in Ghana, African Development Bank, 2010.

CHAPTER THIRTEEN

THE EXPERIENCE OF MALAYSIA

Malaysia is a country in Asia with an area of 329 758 km2, and a population of 28.6 million inhabitants (2010) made up of three ethnic groups: the indigenous people named Bumiputra (59%), the Chinese (32%) and the Indians (9%).

Malaysia became independent in 1957. It is a constitutional monarchy made up of 13 states and governed by a federal parliamentary system. The King (elected every 5 years among the 9 reigning sultans) is the head of the army, but the power is really in the hands of the Prime Minister, the head of government. The country produces rubber, palm oil, petroleum and gas.

In 1960, the Malaysian economy had the same level of development as Uganda. However, since then it has expanded rapidly becoming one of the most efficient countries in South-east Asia.

From 1960 to 1990, the real GDP of the country multiplied by seven with an annual growth of 6.8%. In this time, the country's economy reached a development level similar to that of newly industrialised countries. After the 2008 world crisis, the growth diminished, but recovered in 2010 reaching 7.2%. In 2012 it reached

5.6%[99] and was estimated at 4.7% in 2013, boosted by private investments and the improvement of external trade.

Open to the outside, Malaysia's economy relies strongly on external demand. Manufactured products represent 29% of the GDP and 60% of the country's exports. The country exports mainly electronic material and components, petroleum products, palm oil and wood; it imports electronic and electric material, manufactured goods, chemical products, steel, transport material and food and agricultural products. Against the backdrop of the modernising of the economy, there is macro-economic stability and low inflation, a reduction of inequalities with the distribution of national income and the eradication of absolute poverty.

First phase: 1957-70: an industrialisation and state ownership policy

The economic development has gone through three main phases. The first one stretches from independence in 1957 to the end of the 1960s. In that period the country pursued a policy of industrialisation, and a strong penetration of the State in the agricultural sector as well as in the social and physical infrastructures.

During that period, the economic growth, based on the exportation of primary products, was very stable. And some progress was noticeable in the fight against poverty, especially among the indigenous populations.

In terms of education, the government focused on schooling and prolonging education up to secondary

---

[99] See: France Diplomatie: Presentation of Malaysia, 14/04/2014.

level. Although positive results were attained through this policy, the literacy rate among adults remains poor, i.e. much lower than in the other South-east Asian countries.

1971-85: The new economic policy for the eradication of poverty and the restructuring of society

During the second phase, from 1971 to 1985, a new strategy, known as NEP (New Economic Policy), focused on (i) the eradication of poverty and (ii) the restructuring of Malaysian society in order to reduce the imbalances between the different ethnic groups.

The NEP was basically aiming at improving the Bumiputras' economic position with state intervention to reach this objective. Quotas were implemented to involve indigenous people in the ownership of commercial and industrial companies.

The 1975 Act on industrial coordination made the issuing of licences for the establishment of companies in the country subject to certain quotas for the participation of indigenous people.

Banks, in turn, had to grant loans with interest rebates to priority sectors, including companies held by indigenous people.

At the same time, the State nationalised foreign companies and created new companies to improve Bimuputras' access to executive positions.

At the beginning of the 1980s, with the income from the sale of fuels and gas, the government launched an extensive programme for the setting up of capital-intensive industries through the Heavy Industries Corporation of Malaysia – HICOM for which it provided the initial capital and facilitated access to bank credits at reasonable terms.

In 1988, the state established nine companies, very often in joint-venture with foreign investors.

However, the strong State intervention led to low productivity and a very high corporate debt. Thus in 1988, the deficit of public companies amounted to RM 1 billion.

Third phase (1986-1990): adjustment and liberalization

During the third phase of the NEP (1986/1990), government strove to correct these imbalances through an adjustment and liberalisation programme.

The result was that for 50 years Malaysia has experienced, on average, close to 7% growth per annum.

Wawasan 2020 (Vision 2020)

Privatisation, competitiveness and attracting foreign direct investments (FDIs) as well as the gradual withdrawal of the State from production sectors have become the main axes of the National Development Policy that followed the NEP, and of the Vision 2020 of former Prime Minister, Mohamad Mahatir.

Vision 2020's main objective is to turn Malaysia into a developed country by 2020, Indeed, currently a medium-income country, Malaysia wants to become a developed country with a high income by 2020. This means a GDP per capita of US$15 000 by 2020, against US$8 000 in 2010. "In order to achieve this vision essential structural reforms must be rapidly implemented to increase productivity, domestic and foreign investments, and transform the current drivers of growth to make of Malaysia a country focusing on innovation and higher value-added products".

The new implemented policies have already enabled the country to achieve rapid economic growth since 1986 and to become a leading destination for foreign capital among the new industrialised countries of Asia.

In the last ten years, the GDP growth rate has reached 8.5%. Of course, the last monetary and stock exchange crisis of 1997 has somewhat lowered this figure.

The "new economic model" (NEM), designed to promote innovation and productivity gains was launched together with the tenth five-year plan (2011-2015). The objective of this plan is to double the income per capita by 2020[100].

The keys to success

The rapid growth of the Malaysian economy is due to four main factors:

(i) Physical infrastructures inherited from British domination;

(ii) Foreign direct investments in the manufacturing, service and energy sectors, and the government, and especially the Prime Minister, who acted as catalyst and leader. It is an economic liberalisation without a loss of sovereignty by the State;

(iii) The industrialisation policy (automotive industry) and opening toward external markets.

"The country exports mainly electrical and electronic equipment, machines, mineral fuels and hydrocarbons, oils and animal and plant fats, wood and charcoal. The

---

[100] See: the magazine Lemoci, the engine of international trade, 13/05/2014.

country mainly imports electric and electronic products, machines, fuels and oils, plastic products, iron and steel" [101].

(iv) The high dependence of the economy on a foreign workforce. Under British rule "the pursuit of economic growth was impaired by... a severe labour shortage. To remedy this shortage, the settlers recruited workers in India and China all through the XIX century. This labour immigration had a major impact on the social structure of the country".[102] The indigenous people working in agriculture and the administration are poor and the Chinese working in mines become rich. This segmentation of society paradoxically provided the basis for Malaysia's economic take off. Thus, "on 13 May 1969 political demonstrations, held a few days after the federal elections, degenerated into bloody riots opposing Malaysians to Chinese. After announcing a state of emergency, government implemented a policy to restore social peace and national unity by promoting the enrichment of the Malaysians. The New Economic Policy (NEP) introduced in 1970 is a policy of affirmative action giving Malaysians many privileges: subsidised loans to acquire shares and bonds, priority access to the public service, quota system in higher education and in paid employment in foreign companies, obligation of joint investments with Malaysian businessmen or 'preferential treatment and discriminatory arrangements' in the granting of licences or new companies and preferential access to public markets" [103].

---

[101] See: the magazine Lemoci, quoted already.

[102] Elsa Lafaye de Micheaux, Malaysia, a model of sovereign development?, Lyon, ENS Editions, 2012.

[103] See: Elsa Lafaye de Micheaux , work already quoted.

At the political level, government was flexible in its approach and managed to maintain the difficult balance between growth objectives and the need for justice in the distribution of the national income.

The former Prime Minister, Mahatir, is the main artisan of the economic policy. He is directly responsible for the industrialisation started at the beginning of the 1980s, the strategy consisting of developing commercial relations with Asian countries ("Look East" strategy) and Vision 2020.

In order to assist him, two think tanks operate at the Prime Minister's Office under his direct authority: (i) the Economic Planning Office dealing with economic planning; and (ii) the Coordination and Application Office which has the role of ensuring the coherence and implementation of national and local plans.

Contrary to Thailand, Korea and China, Malaysia started with significant assets (infrastructures, natural resources, especially petroleum).

These natural resources together with political stability enabled the country to attract foreign direct investments (US$6.5 billion in 1996, and the FDI stock in 2012 amounted to US$132 400), to contract massive debts (the external debt represents 30% of the GDP) and to achieve remarkable success in the economic policy. The country is the 3rd recipient of foreign direct investments (FDI) in Asia in 2010, behind Singapore and Indonesia[104].

Although some aspects of its industrialisation policy failed (especially its automotive industry), Malaysia greatly succeeded in its diversification policy of agricul-

---

104 CNUCED (UN Conference on Trade and Development) in his "World Investment Report 2011".

tural products for export (palm oil) and in the electronic industry. "Malaysia is today one of the 20 greatest trading countries in the world. Electronic products are its only and main export category, representing 50% of the total exports of goods in 2005" [105].

And today, it has the economic and social indicators of a country rising to the level of the new industrialised countries. Indeed, within 40 years (1957-1997), the contribution of agriculture to GDP went from 40.7% of GDP in 1960 to less than 20% in 1990; that of the manufacturing industry went from 8% to 35%, that of services from 42 to 45%[106].

The success of the economic and social development policy is due to (i) the environment created by the authorities; (ii) the leadership's determined commitment to set great objectives and control the implementation of the measures taken; (iii) the diversification of its agricultural production: (iv) and taking advantage of the opportunities offered by the international market.

---

[105] Malaysia- European Community, Strategic Document for the period 2007-2013, final Version.

[106] *Malaysia, Social development, poverty reduction and transformation of the economy*, Leong Choon Heng and Tan Siew Hoey.

CHAPTER FOURTEEN

GUINEA IN THIRTY YEARS' TIME

"I believe in materialism. I believe in all the proceeds of a healthy materialism—good cooking, dry houses, dry feet, sewers, drain pipes, hot water, baths, electric lights, automobiles, good roads, bright streets, long vacations away from the village pump, new ideas, fast horses, swift conversation, theatres, operas, orchestras, bands—I believe in them all for everybody".

Francis HACKETT

The Guinean government has already started preparing its: "Guinea, Vision 2035", but unfortunately this long term strategy is still in progress.

When I first discovered the developed countries (or rather the "rich countries"), I experienced an intense shock because I felt the urge to improve this country to the level of those countries. However, the difference between that world and my country was so great that, at first, I thought that catching up would be impossible. Yet, if we mobilised the energies and competences of our society, using the necessary methods and organisation, and a clear vision, even if this may seem utopic, we could manage to do it, as some countries in Asia and Latin America have. Indeed, when faced with a mountain of challenges, you must have a mountain of dreams.

Then, I had a dream in which Guinea emerged as a country where the people were happy with a reasonable standard of living and good education and health systems, highways linking Conakry to Kankan and Kankan to N'Zérékoré, viaducts or tunnels going through the mountains of Foutah Djallon, a high-output agriculture, electricity in towns and villages, theatres, beaches, electrical trains, modern airports, tarred departmental roads, profitable industries, rivers navigable all year round, cinemas showing films in high-definition, etc. The abstraction of this blissful dream gave me a vision called "DYIA 2045" which means happiness or well-being and a protected environment.

In order to make this dream come true, the global strategic objective is to make Guinea a medium-income country (MIC) within 10 to 15 years when the per capita income reaches US$1036 [107], and an emergent country in 20-30 years' time, thus starting in 2034. The challenge to achieve these strategic objectives is huge: achieving an average annual economic growth rate of 8% from 2015, and thereafter a two-figure growth rate. This rate will make it possible to create more wealth and to feed a growing population.

It is estimated that the Guinean population will reach 13.7 inhabitants in 2020. "The period during which the population doubles which was less than 23 years in 1996 will be 24 years in 2020" [108]. On this basis, the population will reach 27.4 million inhabitants in 2044

[107] The World Bank considers that a country has become a middle-income country when the revenue per capita reaches US$1036.

[108] See: Guinea's population: current situation and challenges for the future, Ministry of Planning and UN People Fund, Editions Ganndal, Conakry, May 2013.

and 21.7 million in 2034. It will predominantly be an urban population. As a matter of fact, in 30 years' time, the Guinean population living in towns will be higher than that of those living in villages. It is a universal tendency that is noticed everywhere else. In 1800, only 2% of the world population lived in cities; today, most of the world population is urban[109]. According to Tshwane's Mayor[110], the majority of the demographic growth will be in the towns and cities in poor countries, and from 2020, developing countries will probably be more urban than rural.

To achieve two-figure growth objectives (the unexpected Ebola epidemic will have implications on these perspectives and temporary adjustments will have to be made to mitigate its consequences), the following strategic initiatives will be needed: (i) create the right conditions for public and especially private investment. The investment rate must reach 20% in 2015 and 25% thereafter; (ii) develop the main sources of growth: agriculture, mines (the environmental analysis of the effects of mining must feature prominently), tourism and transport and (iii) conduct strategic actions relating to governance, human resources, regional development and international relations.

[109] See: Tshwane: exemplifying economics of happiness, by Kgosientso Ramokgopa, executive Mayor of Tshwane, in Pretoria News, Tuesday, July 8, 2014.

[110] Tshwane is the indigenous name of Pretoria, capital of South Africa.

1. Strategic actions and big projects

In the fixed time period, a certain number of major projects will have to be planned and implemented that could have a direct influence on improving people's living conditions.

The prerequisites are: implementing transformation measures of agricultural production and developing basic infrastructures necessary to any social and economic development.

Firstly, in this process, the main towns and big villages must have electricity and drinking water 24 hours a day. Secondly, secondary towns and villages must profit from these modern amenities. After 5-10 years, the shortage of electricity, drinking water and load shedding will have much decreased.

The main axes of this huge project strategy will include the following initiatives:

(i) Starting a toll road network; this network will go from Kankan to one part of Forested Guinea, and also to Middle-Guinea and Maritime Guinea. During each five-year presidential mandate, at last one portion of the highway must be completed.

To have an idea of the cost of a dual carriageway between Kankan and Kouroussa, one just has to consult the cost of the road project on the same road recently published in a document of the Ministry of Public Works.

Indeed, there is a road project that was implemented by the French consortium ECIS/SOCETEC in 2012 for the following segments: (i) Mamou-Dabola, 150 km long with a building cost of 151 million Euros: (ii) Dabola-Kouroussa, 160 km long, with a building cost of 124 million Euros. These two segments will require the building of bridges to the cost of 6 million Euros. It will entail a 7m wide roadway and two 1.5m shoulders, and it will therefore be 10m wide.

In addition, to reach Conakry harbour faster and more easily, two ring roads will be built from the 8-November interchange, one ring road on the northern cornice and the other around the southern cornice.

(ii) Building extra airport infrastructures: a large international airport in Maférénya; three international airports in Labé, Kankan and N'Zérékoré in ten years' time.

(iii) Building a large dry harbour in Kankan, which has been planned for many years. These facilities will be warehouses for imports from Mali and from Conakry harbour. Thus in 8 years, these imports will be transported by piggyback to this dry port, thus enabling the Republic of Mali to benefit from cheaper services, compared to the others ports of the sub-region. "The distance Bamako-Abidjan is 1225 km for a transport cost of 43 000 FCFA per ton. On the contrary, the distance Conakry-Bamako, via Kankan is 997 km".[111]

Under the 3rd Republic, towns in the interior were partly equipped with water, electricity, road and capital infrastructures, with the independence celebrations in Boké in 2012 and in N'Zérékoré in 2013. Cuba, in spite of the American embargo, used this strategy for years in another form to implement its main economic objectives. The sector selected by the Cuban authorities received larger budget allocations than the other sectors. Thus there was the sugar cane year, the road year, etc. In the same vein, the first President of Côte d'Ivoire, the

---

[111] See: Mamadi Camara, *Où va la Guinée?* (chapter nine), Editions l'Harmattan, Paris, June 2010.

late Felix Houphouët Boigny, used this strategy best by organising independence celebrations in the big cities of the country alternatively, thus having the opportunity to implement huge socio-economic investments.

The project for the construction of the Conakry-N'Zérékoré railway network,

resources; (iii) putting an end to, or at least considerably called Transguinean, is closer to becoming a reality after half a century of study, design, examination of variations, etc. This railway is currently part of a sub-regional project with the possibility to add two extensions:

- a) Kankan to Bamako via Mandiana and Bououni (in the Republic of Mali)
- b) Kankan to N'Zérékoré Kerouané.

The railway will be an important complement to the road, in transporting goods and passengers at a cheaper cost.

Funding of major projects must be based on the mobilisation of internal and external resources through targeted actions: (i) creating favourable conditions for private national or foreign investment; (ii) mobilising public diminishing political and economic bad governance practices, and exploiting the financial resultant benefits.

Once the conditions have been implemented, several avenues can be explored: (i) mobilising bilateral funds; (ii) mobilising multilateral funds; (iii) mobilising sovereign funds; (iv) mobilising resources coming from the wealth accumulated by individuals or private companies; (v) encouraging foreign direct investments by establishing a business environment favourable to them, etc. Good governance should encourage a massive mobilisation of financial resources. Guinea's mining vocation already attracts the heavy weights of the mining sector. This trend must be strengthened by creating a legal environment which guarantees national and international private investments.

This vision will be implemented through successive five-year development plans. Once the first draft has been developed, we can call on technical assistance to make it a prospective document with precise and well-targeted stages.

II. Strategic political and institutional actions

Revitalisation of political parties and civil society

Democratic institutions will be stronger and more stable. Political parties will be based on a better organisation and a more faithful membership base. And two or more major parties could emerge from the political landscape in order to establish an alternation of power.

In order to do so, political parties must absolutely reorganise their structures and devolve internal power. This reorganisation should be based on a clear choice of leaders, i.e. the election of the President of the Party and one or two vice-presidents through voting. The president of the party then automatically becomes its candidate during the presidential election. This makes it possible to know in advance the different candidates during the forthcoming elections. Ambiguity in this respect has often led the great political parties in French-speaking Africa to collapse into chaos and the loss of power, sometimes irreversibly. This was the case with the Democratic Party of Guinea (PDG) who although it led the country to independence, almost disappeared after President Ahmed Sekou Touré's death in March 1984.

Increased decentralization

Decentralisation must go further with regards to the participation of the people at grass-root level in the exercise of power. In a forward-looking vision, Guinea's four natural regions (Maritime Guinea, Middle-Guinea, Upper Guinea and Forested Guinea) would each be able to elect its Regional Assembly. Furthermore, each Assembly could elect the region's Governor who would yield the executive power at regional level. The implementation of a regional development plan could be the main task of the Government and of its cabinet whose members would be chosen based on their respective expertise. The regional executive could raise some taxes and enjoy discounts from central government.

The executives of these four regions could then positively influence each other in education, health, the building of roads, urbanisation taking into account the preservation of the environment, agricultural production and agro-business. Each region would specialise in the sectors in which it has a comparative advantage.

However, precautions must be taken in the establishment, organisation and exercise of power in the regions. Some prerogatives such as the design and implementation of major projects defence and police will be the responsibility of the central government. Taking into account the mixture of people taking place since the independence of the country, the officials will also be individuals who do not originate from the region in which they live. We must also avoid undermining national unity in the decentralisation process.

Creation of a new capital

Conakry, the present capital, is a peninsula which is like a cul-de-sac. This configuration as well as the uncontrolled settlements means that there is not enough space. Access to Conakry harbour is complicated and resembles an obstacle course at peak time. It would be very expensive to redesign the city and build access roads with the indigenous people not wanting to lose their privileges on their plots of land.

The solution to this problem is to create from scratch a political and administrative capital in the centre of Guinea, not far from Dabola, some 500 km from Conakry, which would be the economic capital of the country. Ecological and modern urbanisation norms would be taken into account to provide the necessary infrastructures: wide streets, suitable electric lampposts for public lighting, green spaces, playgrounds for children, museums, theatres, conference centres, shopping centres, etc. Naturally, buildings will be erected to house republican institutions: the Presidency of the Republic, the National Assembly and the Supreme Court. This new capital could be built with US$3 billion, by investing US$60 million per annum over 5 years.

Take for example the building of the new capital of Nigeria, Abudja, which would originally have amounted to 100 million French francs[112]. "The building of Brasilia, in forty months, is a technological feat, with the transport of construction materials by plane, the work-

[112] See: *Abudja, Cité des rêves, née et morte ...*, by Jean Baumier, in l'Observateur/Economie, 18-24 July 1986. At the rate of 1 French Franc = 0.152 449 017 Euro, 100 billion FF = 15. 245 billion Euros.

ing of reinforced concrete, and acrobatic audacities" [113]. Brasilia was inaugurated in 1960.

Governance and ethics

Central government and regional authorities will operate according to an ethical code covering several aspects, including values such as honesty, expertise and the quality of police records. There will be control systems and the judiciary will play its part. The objective is to prevent as much as possible the temptations of corruption and unlawful behaviour of those with State authority. At a time like ours of excessive media coverage, those who are called upon to lead the country must be role models in safeguarding public funds and leading their private lives.

Those who break the law or the ethical code will be punished according to the law, in order to deter financial offenders or those out of step with morality.

The current practices in public administration, including patronage, misappropriation of public funds and other forms of influence will have stopped, and in their place there will be a more normal functioning based on development. The users of public administration services will not have to follow their dossiers themselves through the administrative circuit to bring them to completion. The State structures will do this work for them and in a fairly short time.

---

[113] See: *Et de nulle part surgit Brasilia*, by Veronique Mortaigne, in Le Monde/Culture et Idées, 16/12/2011.

Education and scientific research

The youth must be well educated from primary school to university. And the administration must stop giving a bad example by promoting the worst employees. Excellence must be commended everywhere in the public and private sectors. Promotion and distinction must go only to the most deserving employees. By doing the opposite, the country's leadership sends a questionable message to the youth who will think it is not necessary to make efforts to succeed at school, thinking that other criteria prevail to get to the top of the State machinery or society.

The strengthening of human resources will play a major role in the years to come. Eight universities will have to be established in the country, namely one per administrative region. These universities will specialise in various branches, giving priority to specialities like the mines, petroleum and the new information technologies.

The plethora of private universities must be reduced to a minimum, namely two or three which will be kept after a very strict assessment of their facilities, the professional body (number of full professors, associate professors and senior lecturers), the quality of practical work workshops and teaching programmes.

The national institute of agricultural research must be better equipped and better used, so that it can become a real test laboratory for farmers. Similarly, the National Institute of Public Health (NIPH) must be situated in a functional building, with suitable research laboratories on endemic diseases like malaria. The NIPH could ask the help of the great research institutes such as CDCs

(Centres for Disease Control and Prevention) of Atlanta, in the Unites States.

III. Culture and Arts

The development of culture gives an indication of the economic and social development of a country. America is not only the first economic power of the world, it is also an essential cultural power.

Guinea will have or create a certain number of institutions or permanent structures to enlarge its culture base, namely:

(i) Creation of a national instrumental and choral

ensemble (there was one in the 1st Republic). This ensemble which used traditional instruments is essential to perpetuate the national culture. The country cannot just have modern orchestras which get their inspiration from abroad. Although this is the century of globalisation in all spheres, each country must present itself on the international market with its own cultural values. The universal civilisation mentioned by Senghor exists today more than ever. However, although rap and soul music are good, the *yankadi* and *mamaya* are just as good.

The ensemble is very important for the sustainability of the musical richness of the cultural heritage of the country: a fusion of mandingue music, polyphonic choirs from Forested Guinea, melodies from Foutah and rhythms from Maritime Guinea.

(ii) Creation of a National orchestra which would perform on official visits to Guinea by distinguished guests. This will showcase the fusions of modern musical instruments with traditional ones and perpetuate the chansons de geste and other melodies of the country's musical heritage.

(iii) Creation of a Music School in each natural region which would teach young people how to play traditional musical instruments such as the *balafon*, *nkoni* with one or two strings, the one string violin of Foutah, the *karian* and the *bölon* (which are starting to disappear from marriage and baptism ceremonies), the *kora* and the *djembe*. It seems that the African Ballets still exist in Guinea. If it is true, we must make this company more visible on the national and international scene.

(iv) Create artistic fortnights once a year to focus people's attention on the arts for two weeks. It will make it possible to periodically regenerate the foundations of our artistic values.

(v) Build theatres in each natural region's Administrative centre; there will be four in total in the interior of the country. These theatres will be places of cultural effervescence which will host the performances of the folk dance groups.

(vi) Make modern movie theatres available in the main cities of the country, showing films in high definition.

IV. Tourism

The tourism industry has become, for many African countries, a source of growth" [114]. Although Guinea has varied natural sites, a diversified climate according to the natural regions and a rich artistic, artisanal and cul-

[114] See: Visa for Mauritius, L'Express No 3125 of 25 May 2011, page 39.

tural heritage, it is late in developing its touristic sector. Badly exploited and heavily handicapped by constraints, tourism could become a growth sector if certain measures were taken and implemented in the medium term.

The bottlenecks include: the lack of facilities, in Conakry as well as in the interior of the country; the lack, even absence, of electricity and a shrinking water supply; the bad road conditions; the lack of air travel links between the natural regions of the country, etc. However, since 2011, hotel accommodation has improved. Classic tourism will rely on the already 301 identified sites. As for business tourism, it will get an injection as investors have come back, especially in the mining sector. The strengthening of these two types of tourism relies strongly on the state of infrastructures and the business environment.

V. Guinea in the family of nations

Regional integration

Since Guinea became independent in 1958, it has strived to help other African countries to gain their independence. In order to do this, it spared neither effort nor trouble, even sending troops to some Portuguese colonies, housing freedom fighters from the African National Congress (ANC) of South Africa, SWAPO from Namibia or the National Liberation front of Algeria (FNLA). Guinea has therefore played a leading role, strongly committed to the liberation struggles of other countries under foreign domination.

After decolonisation, the country fought for African unity. President Ahmed Sekou Touré is one of the founding fathers of the Organisation of African Unity (OAU) which has become today the African Union (AU). Guinea is part of a certain number of sub-regional clusters, the main ones being: the Mano River Union, the OMVS (Senegal River Basin Development Authority), and ECOWAS (Economic Community of West African States). The integration has always been an ongoing concern of the country's leaders, because it is a source of more opportunities and economic development.

The integration of ECOWAS member states will be a more tangible reality, which will materialise, if possible, by creating a common currency which is legal tender in the 16 countries of the Community, with a common market of goods and services and, to avoid the errors noticed in other unions on other continents, a joint budgetary management. This will mean the establishment of a supranational Federal State with a political will which is not a pipe dream.

Besides a political interest, Guinea has an economic interest in sub-regional integration due to the fact that, if it developed a heavy industry one day, based on the rich iron deposits of the country, its demographics and the dimension of its economy and its market would not be enough to absorb the capital goods produced. Thus, when Guinea will develop its large hydroelectric potential, it will become a net exporter of energy.

International relations

The country has always wanted to establish friendly relations with other countries of the world, based on an equal partnership.

At the Unites Nations, it has furthermore always defended Africa's interests, guided by its fierce love of independence and freedom for all people, even if it attracted the enmities of the great powers.

The probable impact of the exploitation of the richness of underground resources.

Taking into account the richness of underground resources, Guinea has established partnerships with great multinational companies; these relations must take into account the interests of each partner and the "win-win" principle. This type of partnership will enable the country to exploit its mining resources to make sure that they will have a definite impact on economic and social development.

We can consider the pessimistic hypothesis that the current situation will not improve much, in case of civil war or recurring social upheavals, as was seen in the period 2001-2010. However, the measures that would mitigate such a hypothesis lie in the fact that republican institutions are in place in Guinea and that the political debate is taking place legally in the National Assembly and the medias. This more or less defuses politically inspired street demonstrations and violence. It preserves the peace necessary for economic and social development.

It is however possible to consider a course without interference which would emerge from an optimistic vision, in other words, a problem-free evolution.

This optimistic vision of an evolution could be based on the discovery of petroleum in a marketable quantity and especially on the medium-term exploitation of iron ore from Simandou. If the retrocession of plots 2 and 3 to Rio Tinto, which was signed on 26 May 2014 by an agreement between the Government and the Australian-English company, leads to effective exploitation in the near future, it will inject US$20 billion into Guinea's economy, including the costs of the exploitation of the iron deposit, the building of a 650 km railways to transport the ore to the Atlantic coast, a harbour deep sea port and 1 000km of roads.

The Simandou railway project by Rio Tinto has the following characteristics:

- Length: 650 km;
- Standard gauge: 1435 mm;
- Axle load: 40 tons;
- 3 tunnels of 24 km in total;
- Number of bridges and viaducts: 68;
- Approximate cost: US$7 086 billion, including rolling stock.

An ore-carrying train will comprise 6 locomotives, 240 waggons and one passenger carriage for the personnel, some 2500 m in length. These estimates will be refined by a bankable feasibility study that the Rio Tinto group will finalise within one year. And standards, will bring something new and original to Simandou will change the economic situation in Guinea. The implementation of the project will have a great impact to which Guinea's economy will have to adapt.

Indeed, the orders will suddenly be so big that it will be difficult to meet them. Resorting to the services of local companies, the massive purchase of vehicles, food and public works vehicles and the application of international medical, BTP and other norms Guinea's economic landscape.

Moreover, according to estimates, Simandou will greatly help boost small and medium size enterprises, mobilise fiscal resources, pay different types of royalties and create 40 000 jobs. The effective start of the project will significantly change the arithmetic of the aggregate growth by inducing a higher growth than the 8% aimed at by the optimistic evolution prospects of the Guinean economy.

In fact, due to Guinea's current GDP growth rate , namely 2.5% registered in 2013, the forecast of the Ministry of Planning is that this rate could double from 2016[115]. It could be a two-figure growth rate at the start of the Simandou production year (2018-2019), i.e. an average of 15% during the first two years.

Under the exploitation of the iron ore of Nimba, of bauxite and maybe oil, the Guinean economy will be in 30 years' time *"the economics of happiness"*, offering the people not only basic infrastructures (drinking water, electricity), but also a high income, a clean environment, free Wi-Fi access, quality public transports, highways between the main cities, tarred roads between prefectures and sub-prefectures, well-maintained dirt roads between sub-prefectures and districts, modern airports in the provincial capitals of the four natural regions, high speed trains between the main cities, a better educated people and communities living in harmony.

The economics of happiness will turn Guinea into an attractive place to live, a country where the different

---

[115] Yet, the growth expectations can be jeopardised by the Ebola virus which is a priority for the government. It will have a definite impact on economic activities which have significantly slowed down, as the borders with certain countries have been closed, and a large part of foreign investors preferring to implement their project later (the meeting of the Prime Minister with the hotel managers in Conakry in August 2014 showed that hotel occupancy decreased to 10%).

parts of the population will be happy, where all the people will have a better quality of life.

In this hypothetical view, the transformation of Guinea into a medium-income country and, later, into an emerging country, will take place faster than expected. And the long-awaited prosperity, desired by the people since the independence of the country in 1958, will finally become a tangible reality.

CONCLUSION

In the years following independence in the 60's, Africa was obviously severely handicapped by the impacts of colonialism and struggled to kick-start its economic and social development. However, since the beginning of the 21st century, the parameters are taking on a new form. As a matter of fact, in the last ten years, there have been high growth rates. On average, Africa's GDP shows a 5% annual growth rate.

According to Carlos Lopes[116], if this growth rate is maintained, projections show that that Africa's GDP will increase threefold by 2030 and sevenfold as from 2050.

Yet, like all averages, it masks large disparities between different countries. In fact, if we take Guinea as an example, before and after the first ten years of independence, the country was unable to reach a growth rate of 6%, the target value proposed in "Guinea, Vision 2010" in 1996.

The lesson that can be drawn from past experiences points to several ingredients of growth and development: industrialisation, creating institutions, stabilisation, promotion of external trade, education, health, structural adjustments, governance, etc.

---

[116] See: article already quoted.

All these approaches must be rethought and development strategies must be initiated from within the country, taking into account each country's own specifications, history and geography. In doing this, we will have to get rid of the colonial economy that turned Africa into the provider of agricultural and mineral raw materials for the industrialised world, in order to create added value for our products.

The basis of these strategies should include a variety of elements: a vision, strategic actions, development plans. Moreover, development requires time, financial resources, local expertise and good governance. A sound combination of all these elements will lead to growth, a strong growth that should reverse the ever-increasing poverty. Development does not go well with improvisation. Catching up with developed countries will only take place at a price.

The quest for development is not a panacea. Each country must design the best strategies for its sociological and political realities, its natural ground and underground resources, its history and culture.

Through well-designed and rigorously implemented economic policies, or due to the positive impact of oil production, some African countries have managed in the last decade to register two-figure growth rates. It enabled them to set up socio-economic infrastructures providing their people with a higher quality of life than in the 60s.

However, on the whole, poor people have benefitted little from the effects of growth. A country like Angola, for instance, recorded a 20.8% growth rate of GDP in 2008, yet over 60% of its people live in extreme poverty[117]. In spite of its oil wealth and its high GDP (the country ranks 66th in the world in terms of GDP), Angola ranks 101st in terms of its GDP per capita. This gives an indication of the overall wealth of the population[118]. Even in Ghana which has had, in the last 6 years, an 8.5% average annual growth rate of GDP, the economic and political successes do not benefit everybody. Having natural resources does not necessarily mean that the majority of the people will enjoy its ensuing benefits.

Although Guinea is a richly endowed mining country, it is not part of these countries. After over 50 years of independence, the economic and social development is slow to take off. There are various reasons for this paradox, relating to the political and economic situation and to the negligence of successive ruling classes, as well as to the international context. Yet, the country has many assets in terms of natural and human resources.

After 56 years of inefficient economic and financial management, and after observing examples of good practices elsewhere in Africa and Asia, it is possible to shape a vision and a strategy of economic and social development for Guinea, based on its natural resources, not just the mines, taking into account globalisation and the opportunities it offers. This strategy that we call Guinea Transformation Strategy (GTS) will ensure the development of human resources and good governance, and will rest on four pillars: agriculture, hydroelectric energy, mining and good governance. These three sectors can become permanent levers to activate a virtuous

---

[117] See: Jeune Afrique No 2765 of 5-11 January 2014.

[118] See: BMF warns SA economy from transformation goal, by Zandisile Luphahla, in the New Age, Thursday, 19 June 2014.

dynamic in economic and social development. They have a great potential of job creation and can generate large internal financial resources and considerable export revenues. Adopting this strategy will demonstrate a real desire to diversify the economy of Guinea.

The links between the four pillars on which Guinea's development will rest are very closely connected. The mining and food industries need a great quantity of electricity to develop. A flourishing agriculture is essential to feed thousands of workers and other experts working in the bauxite and iron ore processing plants. And good governance enables the majority of the population to benefit from the exploitation of agriculture, hydroelectric production and the processing on site of minerals.

However, to get most out of these growth clusters, the State will have, through large allocations of adequate financial resources, to ensure the development of growth accelerators such as education, health and road infrastructures.

BIBLIOGRAPHIE

I. PUBLICATIONS ON GUINEA

La Guinée, sa « terre »: potentiels minier et agricole et son peuple: potentiel humain, by Mr. Denis Thirouin, mining expert, General Secretary of the Mifergui-Nimba company, *in* La Lettre Diplomatique n° 98, Second quarter 2012

2001 Annual macro-economic framework (Implementation of the poverty reduction strategy), Ministry of Planning, National Planning Directorate, (Annexes), Conakry, July 2012

Guinea CPD sector profile mining, a paper presented at the Abu Dhabi Forum, 2013

Ibrahima Soumah, Avenir de l'industrie minière en Guinée, Editions l'Harmattan, Paris, 2006, Table of page XII

National workshop on the context of medium-term public expenditure, Energy sector (Electricity, renewable energy, Water, Hydrocarbons), Ministry of national Resources and Energy, Republic of Guinea, 1997

A synthesis on hydroelectric dams in Guinea, prepared by Ousmane Tanou Diallo, Electrical Engineering Consultant, Energy specialist, 2012

« Souapiti: a promising site for the industrialisation of Guinea and the sub-regional energetic integration »,

Examination of the hydroelectric potential of the Konkoure River, 2012

Report on Guinea’s economic and social situation (2009-2011), Ministry of Planning, National Planning Directorate, Conakry, November 2012.

A major asset for the valorisation of Guinea’s hydroelectric potential. The West African Power Pool (WAPP)/ Le système d'échanges d'énergie électrique ouest-africain (EEEOA), 2012

Guinea: (i) Policy Note on Electricity and Water, Emilio Sacerdoci, Consultant, World Bank, 21 May 2010; (ii) Report on Guinea’s economic and social situation, 2009-2011, Ministry of Planning, National Planning Directorate, Conakry, November 2012

Paper delivered at the Investors Forum in Abu-Dhabi FP Livestock Agriculture GAD, « Investment opportunities in livestock (hatchery, cattle food production, abattoirs, animal selection and crossbreeding)”, December 2013

Guinea’s population: current situation and challenges of the future, Ministry of Planning and UN Population Fund, Editions Ganndal, May 2013

National Agriculture census (RNA: 2000/2001) National Agricultural Statistics Service (SNSA, National Statistics Institute, Republic of Guinea, 28 January 2012

National Agriculture Census (RNA: 2000/2001) National Agricultural Statistics service (SNSA, National Statistics Institute, Republic of Guinea, 28 January 2012: Table entitled: Production dynamics of main subsistence crops from 2000 to 2015, SNSA, Ministry of Agriculture and Livestock breeding

Agriculture in Guinea at the beginning of 2000, by Olivier Bain, article placed on line by Jean-Marc Liotier, in Afrique : histoire, économie , politique 1998- 2001

Mamadi Camara, Quarante ans de gestion socialiste et libérale de la monnaie en Guinée, Editions Ganndal, Conakry, September 2003

Mamadi Camara, Où va la Guinée ? Editions l'Harmattan, Paris, June 2010

Abdou! Goudoussou Diallo, Géographie de la Guinée, Editions l'Harmattan, 2011

Maurice Houis, La Guinée Française, Editions Maritimes et Coloniales, 1953

Article on the hydroelectric development of Kaleta on the Konkoure River, by Ousmane Tano Diallo, Electrical Engineering Consultant, Energy Specialist, September 2012

Document on poverty reducing strategy DSRP III (2013-2015), Ministry of Economy and Finance, permanent Secretariat of the poverty reducing strategy (SP-SRP), May 2013

Poverty and inequalities in Guinea from 1994 to 2012, Analysis from surveys in households, Ministry of Planning, National Planning Directorate, July 2012

II. PUBLICATIONS FROM INTERNATIONAL FINANCIAL INSTITUTIONS

Cape Verde: country files, September 2009, World Bank

Africa's economic prospects in 2012, Cape Verde country file

Evaluation report of the rehabilitation and extension project of the electrical networks of Conakry, Guinea, African Development Bank, July 2008 Guinea: Strategy Document-country (DSP) 2012-2016, African Development Bank, Western regional Department 2, December 2011

Agricultural Sector Strategy of the African Development Bank Group 2010-2014, 7 December 2009

Madagascar: For a dialogue on development challenges, World Bank, June 2013

Global economy to grow this year, World Bank in Business Report, South Africa's national financial daily, Wednesday, January 15, 2014

Madagascar: Economic Update, the World Bank Group . Antananarivo Country Office, October 2012

Ghana: Strategy document - country 2012-2016, African development Bank, 2012

Ghana, Economic prospects in Africa, BAID/OCDE 2007

Economic prospects in Africa 2014, West Africa, Ghana, updated on 06/09/2013

FMI, *World Economic Outlook*, 2013

Cape Verde: Assessment of Bank aid 1996-2007, Department of operations evaluation (OPEV), African Development Bank Group, 15 October 2009

Governance in Africa: State of affairs, in Etudes et Recherches économiques n° 67, by Tchaboure Aime Gogue, FASEG, University of Lomé, African Development Bank

Guinea, Assessment report of the economic and financial reforms support programme (PAREF), African development Bank, March 2011

Guinea: Strategy document - country 2012-2016, prepared by ORWB, African Development Bank, 26 January 2012

World Bank report 2000-2001 on development titled "Fighting poverty", World Bank, September 2000

III. OTHER PUBLICATIONS

Rene Dumont, L'Afrique noire est mal partie, Editions du Seuil, Paris, 1962

Paul Samuelson, l'Economique, tome 2, Editions Armand Colin, Paris, 1975

Dictionnaire d'économie et de sciences sociales, 7th reviewed Edition, expanded, edited by C.D. Echaudermaison, Editions Nathan, Paris, 2007

Samir Amin, La faillite du développement en Afrique et dans le tiers-monde. Une analyse politique, Editions l'Harmattan, Paris 1989

Paul Vi, Populorum, 1957

Malaysia: Social development, reduction of poverty and transformation of the economy, Leong Choon Heng and Tan Siew Hoey

Economic and historical analysis of contemporary societies, Philippe Deubel, Pearson Education, France, 2008

CNUCED (UN Conference on Commerce and Development) in its « World Investment Report 2011 »

Political History, drawn from the booklet "Ghana - a brief guide", published by the Ghana Information Services Department, 1994

Michel Lesourd, Insularism and Development in the Republic of Cape Verde, Laboratory for the Study of arid regions, University of Rouen, February 1994

Markus Eberhardt and Francis Teal, « Ghana and Côte d'Ivoire: a role reversal », in International Development Policy, Revue internationale de politique de développement, January 2010

Chukwu-emeka Chikezie Chukwu-emeka Chikezie, the African Diaspora: pan-Africanism or village solidarity? Paper presented in the third Forum for the development of Africa (ADF III), « Defining priorities of regional integration », UN Conference Centre, Addis-Ababa (Ethiopia), AFFORD 3 - 8 March 2002

Ghana, Economic prospects in Africa, BAfD/OCDE 2007

Economic prospects in Africa 2014, West Africa, Ghana, updated on 06/09/2013

Ghana and Côte d'Ivoire : a role reversal, International development policy/Revue internationale de la politique de développement (online), by Markus Ehrhardt and Francis Teal, both researchers at the Oxford University, 24 January 2014

Iza Lejarraga, the purring tiger or the meowing cat: diagnostic study of growth in Ghana, African Development Bank, 2010

Official document of the Conference of member countries of the Alliance of Cocoa producing countries (Copal), who met in Yaounde, Cameroon, on 08-12 October 2012 for their 75th General Assembly

Malaysia-European Community, Strategic document for 2007-2013, final version.

Elsa Lafaye de Micheaux, Malaisie, un modèle de développement souverain?, Lyon, ENS Editions, 2012

The improvement of the Governance of large scale financial investments in Africa: the role of parliamentarians, by Dr. Joan C. Kagwanja, Responsible for the land policy Initiative – the regional integration and the trade division – Economic Commission for Africa (CEA), 6th annual Conference of the Presidents of the National Assemblies and Senates of Africa, 13-14 August 2014, Midrand, Johannesburg, Republic of South Africa.

IV. JOURNALS AND MAGAZINES

Visa for Mauritius, L'Express n° 3125 of 25 May 2011, page 39.

Interview given by Mory Diane, Vice-President of Amex International, a maritime brokerage firm, on the programme « Plus d'Afrique » of Radio France Internationale on Saturday, 10 November 2012, programme presented by Alain Foka in which he presents men and women who show what Africa is capable of.

La croissance pour tous, c'est possible, in Jeune Afrique n° 2765 of 5- 11 January 2014

Celestine ZANOU, « From the Lagos Action Plan (PAL) to NEPAD : two development concepts, two ideologies .... » in La Presse du Jour of 12 December 2008

Focus I : Funding for Africa's Development

De nouveaux outils pour financer les défis d'une nouvelle Afrique, by Henri de Raincourt, Minister of

Cooperation, and Donald Kaberuka, President of the African Development Bank, in Le Monde of 25/04/2011

Le Quotidien du Peuple in line, Edition of 16-10-2007

Ghana, a rising star in African Business, n° 395 March 2013

"Scaling up agribusiness should be Africa's next growth frontier", by Pedro Lopes, Executive Secretary of the UN Economic Commission for Africa, in Business Report International, Johannesburg, in the section Opinion and Analysis, Thursday, April 17, 2014

Good news India, from famine to plenty, from humiliation to dignity, November 2002, on line

Agency Ecofin Agro of 16 April 2013

Laurent Curau, Fondateur@cafedela brousse.com, on 19 November 2012, from the World Gold Council publications

The Lemoci magazine, le moteur du commerce international, 13/05/2014

France Diplomatie, Presentation of Malaysia, 14/04/2014

Abuja, Cité des rêves, née et morte ...in l'Observateur/Economie, by Jean Baumier, 18-24 July 1986

Et de nulle part surgit Brasilia, in Le Monde/Culture et Idées, 16/12/2011, by Véronique Mortaigne

BMF warns SA economy far from transformation goal, by Zandisile Luphahla, in The New Age (South African daily), Thursday, 19 June 2014

Tshwane : exemplifying economics of happiness, by Kgosientso Ramokgopa, executive mayor of Tshwane, in Pretoria News, Tuesday, July 8, 2014

Guinée-Conakry

aux éditions L'Harmattan

Dernières parutions

INDÉPENDANCE (L') DE LA GUINÉE EN 1958
Chronologie et commentaires
Keita Sidiki Kobélé
L'auteur de ce livre a choisi l'année 1958, l'une des plus controversées de l'histoire de l'indépendance guinéenne, pour démontrer ses théories : l'histoire véritable doit refuser de céder sa place à la légende, à l'affabulation, aux chroniques arrangées. Elle doit, pour ce faire, exiger l'approfondissement des recherches documentaires afin de mieux appréhender tous les tenants et les aboutissants ou tous les aspects d'un fait.
(25.00 euros, 252 p.)
ISBN : 978-2-343-04646-4, ISBN EBOOK : 978-2-336-36704-0

TOURBILLON (LE) VERS LA SORTIE
Barry Aminata
Ce troisième épisode de *Tourbillon* marque le point final d'un vécu décrit dans une tourmente politico-sociale. L'auteur a voulu être le témoin d'une histoire, la sienne, qui s'est déroulée en Guinée.
(Coll. Harmattan Guinée, 14.00 euros, 136 p.)
ISBN : 978-2-343-05387-5, ISBN EBOOK : 978-2-336-36797-2

FORMATION INITIALE DES MAÎTRES EN GUINÉE ET ENJEUX DE LA SCOLARISATION PRIMAIRE UNIVERSELLE
Diané Baba - Préface Hadja Aida Bah Diallo
Ce livre tente d'apporter des réponses à plusieurs questions que soulève l'introduction, dans le système guinéen de formation des maîtres, d'un programme novateur. Des interrogations fondamentales se posent pour baliser le dispositif de formation des instituteurs. Ce livre questionne le processus d'administration du modèle en termes d'efficacité interne et externe, de pertinence, de cohérence, d'apprentissage et de transfert.
(Coll. Harmattan Guinée, 25.00 euros, 246 p.)
ISBN : 978-2-343-05098-0, ISBN EBOOK : 978-2-336-36433-9

MON CAHIER DE MORALE
Cours de morale dispensés par Germaine Legoff à l'ENRJF de Rufisque (1944-1945)
Bah Hadja Nima - Préface de Boubacar Diallo
En ce début de XXIe siècle, la Guinée traverse une crise sociale, politique, économique et culturelle d'une ampleur sans précédent. Ce constat atteste qu'il

y a un déficit en matière d'éducation civique et morale (ECM). Face à cette situation, l'auteur, ancienne Rufisquoise, apporte son expérience de «legoffienne». Elle met à notre disposition son cahier de morale de l'École Normale Supérieure de jeunes filles de Rufisque. Ces cours ont été conduits de main de maître par Germaine Legoff, l'éducatrice mythique.
(Coll. Harmattan Guinée, 11.50 euros, 86 p.)
ISBN : 978-2-343-03333-4, ISBN EBOOK : 978-2-336-36315-8

ÉDUCATION (L') SEXUELLE EN ISLAM
Fofana Mory
L'éducation sexuelle ou, mieux, «l'éducation au mariage», est un commentaire des principaux hadiths sur la question du mariage légitime en islam. On y parle du modèle de femme à épouser, de la dot, de l'accouchement, du baptême, et du calendrier mensuel du couple. Les solutions qu'on y préconise face aux différents problèmes du couple sont de nos jours pour la plupart confirmées par les données de la science. Un ouvrage pour tous ceux qui nourrissent le désir d'être bien informés sur la délicate question de la vie à deux.
(Coll. Harmattan Guinée, 10.00 euros, 102 p.)
ISBN : 978-2-343-03560-4, ISBN EBOOK : 978-2-336-36389-9

LETTRE DE POLITIQUE NATIONALE, DE DÉCENTRALISATION ET DE DÉVELOPPEMENT LOCAL 15 JUIN 2011
***Suivie de* Plan d'action pour la mise en œuvre de la lettre de politique nationale, de décentralisation et de développement local 15 juin 2010**
Ministère de l'Administration du Territoire et de la Décentralisation
Préface d'Alhassane Condé
La LPN-DDL représente le cadre conceptuel, juridique et institutionnel de la politique de l'État dans les domaines précis de la décentralisation et de la déconcentration. Elle se place au cœur de la réforme de l'État. Sa mise en œuvre permettra de créer, autour des collectivités locales, des pôles de développement économique dynamiques et structurés, et de diffuser plus efficacement le développement local à l'intérieur du pays.
(Coll. Harmattan Guinée, 20.00 euros, 186 p.)
ISBN : 978-2-343-03366-2, ISBN EBOOK : 978-2-336-36365-3

DÉMON TAUREAU
Contes de Guinée-Conakry
Diallo Boubacar
Comment un chasseur réussit-il à tromper le diable ? Comment Kirdi, un grand séducteur, perdit-il son pénis ? Comment Hammadi réussit-il à vaincre Démon Taureau ? Comment Salé fut-elle transformée en mouche ? Le lecteur trouvera les réponses dans ce recueil de contes initiatiques amusants mais parfois tragiques et fera un beau voyage, passant par le Soumbouya et la Mellacorée, les montagnes, les forêts galeries et les bowé du Fouta Djallon, la savane du Mandé, la forêt dense du Nimba...
(Coll. La légende des mondes, 12.00 euros, 110 p.)
ISBN : 978-2-343-04589-4, ISBN EBOOK : 978-2-336-36055-3

TRANSITIONS (LES) POLITIQUES EN GUINÉE
De son indépendance à 2010
Bah Ibrahima - Préface de Dominique Bangoura
Depuis son indépendance en 1958, la Guinée a connu plusieurs types de transitions politiques. La première, post Sékou Touré, s'est terminée par la prise du pouvoir par l'armée (1984). Après un régime d'exception de six ans, la Guinée s'engage dans une nouvelle transition. Cependant, l'ère démocratique fut éphémère. Après une tentative de renversement du pouvoir par des militaires en 1996, le régime de Lansana Conté bascula dans l'autoritarisme jusqu'à sa mort en 2008, suivie d'un putsch militaire dirigé par le capitaine Moussa Dadis Camara. Après une tentative d'assassinat du capitaine Camara, le général Sékouba Konaté conduisit cette transition à l'élection présidentielle de juin et novembre 2010.
(Coll. Afrique : politiques publiques, sécurité, défense, 26.00 euros, 256 p.)
ISBN : 978-2-343-00606-2, ISBN EBOOK : 978-2-296-53884-9

CONAKRY : LA RÉPUBLIQUE DES VOLEURS
Bah Thierno
Dès ses premiers discours à la nation après son installation à la tête de la Guinée, Conté déclare : «Nous sommes arrivés pauvres au pouvoir. Si vous nous voyez construire des villas et acheter des voitures, c'est que nous avons volé.» Arrivé au pouvoir à partir de 1990, il prend goût à l'argent. Il installe son régime dans le pillage illimité des richesses nationales. Il favorise le détournement des devises. À la fin de sa vie, sa fortune a été estimée à 450 millions de dollars.
(38.00 euros, 380 p.)
ISBN : 978-2-336-29345-5, ISBN EBOOK : 978-2-296-53307-3

DESTINS GUINÉENS
Mémoires d'un rescapé du goulag de Sékou Touré
Touré Tura Arafanour Naby-Moussa
Face à des horreurs inimaginables du goulag de Sékou Touré et de son régime barbare qui a sévi en Guinée pendant plus d'un quart de siècle, l'auteur raconte le miracle de sa propre survie. Il rend hommage à ses compagnons à travers une galerie de personnalités et d'anonymes torturés dans les camps de la mort. Ce témoignage a pour but d'accomplir un devoir de mémoire et d'honorer tous ceux qui ont comblé les innombrables fosses communes.
(Coll. Harmattan Guinée, 27.00 euros, 266 p.)
ISBN : 978-2-343-00098-5, ISBN EBOOK : 978-2-296-53164-2

MIGRATIONS, ONG ET DÉVELOPPEMENT EN GUINÉE
Barry Idrissa
Voici une analyse de la migration guinéenne, au croisement des enjeux économiques, politiques et culturels. Les rapports migration/développement en Guinée sont étudiés dans plusieurs domaines : transferts matériels et culturels, participation de la diaspora, développement participatif, rapport entre Guinéens de l'intérieur et de l'extérieur, clivages et influences politiques.
(Coll. Études africaines, 23.00 euros, 218 p.)
ISBN : 978-2-336-29212-0, ISBN EBOOK : 978-2-296-53148-2

MARIO, LE BASKET-BALL ET MOI
Mario vu et raconté par Leah
Diallo Alpha Leah
Par le sport et dans le sport naquit une amitié, entre Leah et Mario, les basketteurs de l'équipe nationale de Guinée. L'amitié est la seule raison qui a poussé Leah à consacrer un livre à son compère Mario, le fabuleux numéro 10, le prince charmant du basket-ball guinéen, afin qu'il vive éternellement.
(Coll. Harmattan Guinée, 25.00 euros, 246 p.)
ISBN : 978-2-336-00933-9, ISBN EBOOK : 978-2-296-51635-9

TOURBILLON (LE)
Le combat
Barry Aminata
Faisant suite à un premier volume *Tourbillon, la dérive autoritaire*, ce livre est un feuilleton, celui de la vie de l'auteur, sur un certain parcours fait d'épines et de pétales, avec comme fil conducteur la responsabilité politique du fait d'autrui.
(Coll. Harmattan Guinée, 14.00 euros, 136 p.)
ISBN : 978-2-336-00918-6, ISBN EBOOK : 978-2-296-51634-2

CONTES DE LA BROUSSE, DE LA FORÊT, DE LA SAVANE ET DE LA MONTAGNE
Diallo Boubacar
Ce livre présente les contes de toutes les régions naturelles de la Guinée, sans aucune forme de discrimination. Il s'agit donc d'un survol des aires culturelles de la Guinée avec, en toile de fond, les histoires tissées autour du prince des arbres, le kouratier. C'est un arbre aux vertus multiples qui donne ses fruits à manger, son ombre, du bois mort, des médicaments traditionnels et, aussi, des récits féériques.
(Coll. Harmattan Guinée, 9.50 euros, 58 p.)
ISBN : 978-2-336-00932-2, ISBN EBOOK : 978-2-296-51633-5

ÉCONOMIE (L') POLITIQUE DE LA GUINÉE (1958-2010)
Des dictatures contre le développement
Cournanel Alain
La République de Guinée a subi en cinquante ans deux types de régime, deux formes de dictature. La Ire République (1958-1984), dirigée par Sékou Touré, a sacrifié le développement de la jeune nation à l'omnipotence du parti unique aux mains d'un noyau inamovible. La IIe République (1984-2008), dictature molle à peine déguisée en État de droit, a confié le pouvoir d'État aux prétoriens et l'orientation économique au FMI.
(Coll. Etudes africaines, 31.00 euros, 296 p.)
ISBN : 978-2-296-99810-0, ISBN EBOOK : 978-2-296-51374-7

L'Harmattan Italia
Via Degli Artisti 15; 10124 Torino
harmattan.italia@gmail.com

L'Harmattan Hongrie
Könyvesbolt ; Kossuth L. u. 14-16
1053 Budapest

L'Harmattan Kinshasa
185, avenue Nyangwe
Commune de Lingwala
Kinshasa, R.D. Congo
(00243) 998697603 ou (00243) 999229662

L'Harmattan Congo
67, av. E. P. Lumumba
Bât. – Congo Pharmacie (Bib. Nat.)
BP2874 Brazzaville
harmattan.congo@yahoo.fr

L'Harmattan Guinée
Almamya Rue KA 028, en face
du restaurant Le Cèdre
OKB agency BP 3470 Conakry
(00224) 657 20 85 08 / 664 28 91 96
harmattanguinee@yahoo.fr

L'Harmattan Mali
Rue 73, Porte 536, Niamakoro,
Cité Unicef, Bamako
Tél. 00 (223) 20205724 / +(223) 76378082
poudiougopaul@yahoo.fr
pp.harmattan@gmail.com

L'Harmattan Cameroun
BP 11486
Face à la SNI, immeuble Don Bosco
Yaoundé
(00237) 99 76 61 66
harmattancam@yahoo.fr

L'Harmattan Côte d'Ivoire
Résidence Karl / cité des arts
Abidjan-Cocody 03 BP 1588 Abidjan 03
(00225) 05 77 87 31
etien_nda@yahoo.fr

L'Harmattan Burkina
Penou Achille Some
Ouagadougou
(+226) 70 26 88 27

L'Harmattan Sénégal
10 VDN en face Mermoz, après le pont de Fann
BP 45034 Dakar Fann
33 825 98 58 / 33 860 9858
senharmattan@gmail.com / senlibraire@gmail.com
www.harmattansenegal.com

L'Harmattan Bénin
ISOR-BENIN
01 BP 359 COTONOU-RP
Quartier Gbèdjromèdé,
Rue Agbélenco, Lot 1247 I
Tél : 00 229 21 32 53 79
christian_dablaka123@yahoo.fr

Achevé d'imprimer par Corlet Numérique - 14110 Condé-sur-Noireau
N° d'Imprimeur : 124926 - Dépôt légal : janvier 2016 - *Imprimé en France*

www.ingramcontent.com/pod-product-compliance
Lightning Source LLC
LaVergne TN
LVHW021220061026
849535LV00008B/2830